C000155393

THE JOURNEY FROM EGO TO SOUL

HOW TO TRANSFORM YOUR LIFE WHEN EVERYTHING FALLS APART

KAREN WYATT MD

unroom
tudios

The Journey from Ego to Soul:

How to Transform Your Life When Everything Falls Apart

by Karen Wyatt MD

Published by Sunroom Studios

PO Box 5070

Dillon CO 80435

EBook ISBN: 978-0-9826855-7-0

Print ISBN: 978-0-9826855-6-3

For Larry, Aaron and Gia who brighten my journey every day.

CONTENTS

INTRODUCTION

You lack a foot to travel?
Then journey into yourself —
that leads to transformation of dust into pure gold.

-RUMI

Rumi's verse sums up the primary message of this book: when everything in your life is falling apart and "you lack a foot to travel," an opportunity opens to take an *inward journey* that will reveal who you really are and lead ultimately to your transformation. It may sound simple but the journey Rumi describes can last an entire lifetime and require you to give up everything you have known in the process.

We spend much of the time and energy of our lives focusing on the *outward* journey: choosing and preparing for a career, earning a living wage, and developing relationships to sustain us. But for each person at some point in life there comes an opportunity to begin an *inward* journey where the task involves growing spiritually into our best and highest selves. Often this opportunity to look within arrives as a result of a challenge or crisis or tragedy.

This book depicts such a journey with all of its stages and lessons and obstacles and will serve as a guide for those who are in the middle of falling apart and wondering how to take the next step. The *inward journey* presented here is the story of my own travel into myself and the steps that moved me gradually closer to the "transformation of dust into pure gold." I share my struggles along with the wisdom I have acquired in hopes that they will be an inspiration or a support for your personal journey, even though we each travel very different paths.

Through the stories and lessons on these pages you will learn why it's necessary to *dig deep* into your own Shadow in order to grow, how to cultivate *fearless love* as life unfolds, and how to recognize your own *True Self* or *Soul* as you begin to master your mind and ego. These steps will become familiar with each new story as we spiral again and again through the lessons of the *inward journey*. But the journey itself begins, always, with falling apart and the "perfect storm" that leads to the crisis as in this amazing story:

Neuroanatomist Jill Bolte Taylor was studying brain function at a lab in Boston when at the age of 37 she suffered a massive stroke due to the hemorrhage of a blood vessel in the left side of her brain. As a result of the stroke she lost the ability to speak, read, write and walk and had to spend eight years rehabilitating from the devastating damage to her brain.

This is the type of crisis from which many people might not recover; many might give up and sink into despair for the rest of their lives. Jill Bolte Taylor could have been overwhelmed by the severity of her stroke and the near impossibility of rehabilitation. But as a scien-

tist who had devoted her career to studying the brain, Bolte Taylor was one person who could actually appreciate the irony of this crisis and accept it as a learning opportunity.

In her popular TED talk[1] she said: "I realized, 'Oh my gosh! I'm having a stroke! I'm having a stroke!' The next thing my brain says to me is, 'Wow! This is so cool! How many brain scientists have the opportunity to study their own brain from the inside out?'"

With that realization, Bolte Taylor took a step onto the path of her own inward journey. She remained a student throughout her healing process and gained groundbreaking insights into the functioning of both the left and right hemispheres of the brain. When she finally recovered her ability to speak and write she published a book about her experience titled "My Stroke of Insight: A Brain Scientist's Personal Journey." She gave a TED talk about her story that went viral on the internet in 2008 and then her book became a New York Times Bestseller.

Next she was named to Time Magazine's list of the 100 Most Influential People in the World, appeared on Oprah Winfrey's Soul Series, and then went on to found a non-profit foundation dedicated to providing education and awareness about brain injury and recovery. Also, as a result of the trauma to the left hemisphere of her brain she experienced an enhancement of her right brain function. She discovered previously untapped artistic abilities that have inspired her to create beautiful stained glass replicas of, appropriately, the human brain.

Jill Bolte Taylor is now living a life she could not have imagined one moment before her stroke occurred or during all the years of her lengthy recovery. But she accepted her inward journey when the path was offered to her in the midst of crisis and she has gone on to change the world in remarkable ways.

This story perfectly illustrates the power of the inward journey when it has been embraced and the first step has been taken on that path, even when the outcome is uncertain and there are no guarantees of success or survival. This is the opportunity that becomes available to each of us after everything falls apart if we are courageous enough to dig deep, move into our pain, and allow our lives to be forever changed.

THE BUTTERFLY PRINCIPLE

But why, you might wonder, is it necessary for things to fall apart before this journey can take place? The answer lies in the life cycle of the butterfly, where "falling apart" is an essential and natural step in the process.

Recall that every butterfly begins as a caterpillar, an unappealing, many-legged creature whose only purpose is to eat as much as possible until it can no longer fit inside its own skin. After 4 or 5 cycles of shedding its old restrictive skin, the caterpillar finally stops eating, dangles from a branch and spins a protective cocoon around itself to create a safe space to rest and digest all the food that has been consumed. But that's when everything begins to fall apart for the caterpillar.

Inside the chrysalis the caterpillar has formed a dramatic transformation is taking place, even though it is invisible to an outside observer. In a turn of events that is catastrophic for the caterpillar, its body slowly dissolves away in order to allow a new form to arise. During this destruction of the caterpillar form, previously dormant precursor cells called *imaginal cells* gradually develop and migrate together to create the butterfly that will ultimately emerge.

So the falling apart of the caterpillar is a necessary occurrence in the life journey of the butterfly. Lao Tzu wrote "What the caterpillar calls the end of the world, the master calls the butterfly." We tend to look at our own experiences of falling apart as the end of the world because we cannot imagine the butterfly that is being formed in the process.

According to Maya Angelou: "We delight in the beauty of the butterfly, but rarely admit the changes it has gone through to achieve that beauty." We would like to believe that we are already butterflies and don't need to go through a caterpillar stage in our development. This is one of the follies of the ego that we will learn about in the chapters of this book. We may believe that we can refuse to enter the cocoon and face the falling apart that lies ahead, but ultimately that strategy will fail. We may expect to simply fly past our difficulties, but we will be crushed to learn that our wings have not yet developed.

This book is about embracing the cocoon and allowing the falling apart that needs to happen in our lives so that we can discover our best and most beautiful selves. Remember the butterfly whenever you start to feel discouraged.

MY INWARD JOURNEY

In my own story as you will learn, my father's sudden death by suicide was the crisis that caused my life to fall apart. My struggle to heal from grief and guilt was the beginning of my inward journey as I ultimately found my way to begin working as a hospice doctor. There I was able to learn about death, dying and grief from my hospice patients and their families and gradually heal my own brokenness. Eventually I wrote the book *What Really Matters* (now retitled: *7 Lessons for Living from the Dying*) to chronicle the spiritual lessons I learned at the bedsides of the dying.

This book *The Journey from Ego to Soul: How to Transform Your Life When Everything Falls Apart* is based on my experiences while offering medical care as a volunteer at a domestic violence shelter. That little clinic served as a "laboratory" of sorts for me as I worked to put to use those spiritual principles I had initially learned in hospice. As part of my inward journey of healing from my father's suicide I still had a great deal of work to do in order to master and live by those lessons for living life from higher consciousness.

You will see through the stories in this book how I was confronted by the limitations of my mind and ego and how my Soul gently whispered guidance to me over and over again. As I spiraled through each of the 7 lessons I had learned from my hospice patients I had to dig deep into my own Shadow and heal old wounds before the journey could continue. But with each step I took along that path my True Self was revealed and empowered more and more to become the guidance system for my life.

Ultimately this book is intended to be a companion to *7 Lessons for Living from the Dying,* much as a guidebook is a perfect and necessary companion for a map when you set off on a journey to unfamiliar territory. Though, unlike *7 Lessons,* this book does not focus on the dying process, my intent is to demonstrate how to live a life that is *informed* and *shaped* by the knowledge of our mortality and the fact that everything, sooner or later, falls apart.

This is the essence of the inward journey: traversing the deserts and jungles of loss and dissolution to find the way to a new existence, to the "transformation of dust into pure gold."

THE 7 LESSONS OF THE JOURNEY

7 Lessons for Living from the Dying explains the spiritual lessons I learned from my dying patients and *The Journey from Ego to Soul* provides an example of how those lessons can be applied to daily life in order to live from the Soul rather than the ego. The next chapter of this book will explain how to prepare for your own inward journey and then each of the following 7 lessons will be explored in the subsequent chapters.

Lesson 1: Suffering

The *inward journey* always begins with the lesson of *suffering* because the ultimate purpose of the journey is to learn how to rise above suffering with love. The other 6 lessons contribute to the reinterpretation of suffering so that our very idea of it changes throughout the journey. We will arrive at the end of our explorations with a new understanding of suffering and with new tools for coping with whatever arises in life from that point on. The ego struggles with suffering because it seems unfair and undeserved but this is a crucial lesson. Our failure to embrace the difficulties of life keeps us stuck in lower mind and unable to grow.

Lesson 2: Love

Fearless love is the ultimate lesson of the inward journey that emerges when the Soul, the source of Divine Love, gradually becomes the guiding force of life. But the ego has its own struggle with love throughout the journey as it learns how to be in relationship with others. To move from *selfish love* to genuine *self-love* is part of the challenge that takes place during this lesson. There is a dawning awareness of the full spectrum of love that reaches far beyond the boundaries of romance or infatuation.

Lesson 3: Forgiveness

Once we set out to learn to love others deeply the need for the tool of forgiveness becomes apparent. This lesson can take years to learn and life provides abundant opportunities to practice as we experience disappointment, betrayal, and rejection over and over again. But the practice of forgiveness is essential in order to leave behind the wounds of the past, clear out old resentments, and make space within for more love and creativity.

Lesson 4: The Present Moment

When forgiveness becomes a regular practice, energy that has been stuck in the past, keeping old resentments alive, becomes available in the present moment. We are then able to truly appreciate the beauty, joy, love, and miracles that exist only in this moment. The task of this lesson is to learn how to balance in the present and keep our attention right here, right now rather than being pulled into regrets over the past or worries about the future.

Lesson 5: Purpose

The ego learns an entirely new definition of purpose during this lesson, which challenges all of the goals and intentions that had previously been set for life. Here our life's purpose unfolds in the present moment, where we are now able to fully bring our attention. We recognize that our true "hope" for the future depends only on how well we are able to live and manifest our highest potential in this very moment.

Lesson 6: Surrender

With all of the previous lessons available as tools—love, forgiveness, presence, and purpose—the ego now begins the difficult process of learning to surrender more fully to the guidance of the Soul. The inward journey becomes quite challenging as the ego faces more and more difficulties in order to practice surrender over and over again. But this is essential training for what lies ahead on the path.

Lesson 7: Impermanence

In this final step the ego learns to embrace what it fears the most: that everything changes, that ego has no control over anything, and that nothing lasts except Love. As we finally recognize that the Soul, which is *fearless love* in action, is the only part of us that will not die, we learn to face up to physical death, and the death of the ego, with curiosity and courage. We ultimately see that only the Soul can guide us through the terrifying passageway of physical death and lead us to the Love that we have been seeking all along.

These are the 7 lessons that have transformed my life and have the potential to change how we live in this world of suffering, strife and falling apart. Taken individually, each of these lessons could be the subject of years of study. But together they form a framework for how we can gradually come to recognize the presence of our own Soul and begin to relax into the infinite *fearless love* that exists in that still realm of our own higher consciousness. Any path we choose to follow, any task we wish to complete, any relationship we long to deepen will be served by simply acknowledging these lessons and opening our minds and hearts to learning their wisdom.

Ultimately the learning opportunities will come to us—we don't have to seek them out. Life's curriculum is constantly unfolding, moment-by-moment, and to learn and grow we need only an open heart and mind and a willingness to dig deep within when required. On our spiral path through life we will return over and over again to these 7 lessons, meeting them each time with new awareness, new understanding and new battle scars from our previous challenges.

Perhaps everything has fallen apart in your life, too, for inevitably we each will encounter a crisis that brings us to our knees, dismantles everything we thought we knew and jettisons us back to the beginning to start our life journey anew.

This book is written for all who are seeking wisdom and answers for the unanswerable questions of life. This is for everyone who wonders how to go on with life when everything is falling apart.

But the book is also for those who support and teach others who are suffering. You may find some of the perspectives and tools presented here useful as you work with students and clients. And you may find that as a teacher you are also on your own inward journey while you offer help to other travelers on this road of life.

The Journey from Ego to Soul is here to remind even those who have been spiritual seekers for a long time that a true shift in consciousness requires a journey deep within, initiated by a crisis; a journey that is fraught with challenges, obstacles and downturns. Look inside, dig deep and seek out all remnants of ego where it masquerades as enlightenment, higher wisdom, and emptiness. Be rigorously honest with yourself as you uncover the thin threads of attachment that prevent your full transformation.

No matter how much wisdom you have attained throughout your lifetime, humble yourself and return to your beginner's mind. Put on your walking shoes and begin a simple inward journey, one step at a time, one manifestation of love at a time. This is the path that leads where you want to be right now, but you will have to be patient, for this journey unfolds gradually in its own time. Always, always act from *fearless love*, which is the only thing that really matters on this journey from ego to Soul.

ONE MORE THING ...

A year or so after *What Really Matters* was first published I received an email from a reader who said that when she initially tried to read the book she became so intensely angry that she threw it across the room. Later she shoved it into the back of her closet, vowing never to pick it up again.

It's possible that you might feel that way at times when you're reading *this* book. To be honest even *I* have had those feelings off and on while I've been editing and recording this material. You see, the ego can't stand to be exposed and will react with anger and defensiveness whenever that happens. It will judge, mock and argue with any information that is too painful to look at, then push it away rather than deal with the truth. In my own case, there are days when I can see the limitations of my ego clearly and other days when my vision becomes cloudy again and I get lost in my negative emotions. That's all part of the process so don't be surprised if it happens to you too.

But the reader I mentioned above went on to say that several months after her outburst of anger, her uncle died unexpectedly. In the midst of the devastating grief that she and her family were dealing with, she remembered the book and dug it out of the closet. This time she was able to read it from a different perspective—with a heart that had been broken by grief. Now every word rang true and she found comfort there rather than anger.

So put this book away for awhile if you can't stand reading parts of it. You'll know when you're ready to dig it out again and see it with new eyes. You can read the chapters that feel most in alignment with where you are and skip over those that cause a disturbance. But make note of the resistance you feel because that might show you some Shadow issues that need your attention in the future.

I'm sending you all my love as you undertake this challenging inward journey!

Karen

October 2020

HOW TO USE THIS BOOK

T his book is meant to be a guide to accompany you on a spiritual journey where you transcend your ego and recognize your True Self. My own journey is depicted through one continuous story of my work in a free clinic that introduces each of the 7 lessons. You will read about my struggles, misunderstandings, frustrations, and detours as I worked my way through the task of incorporating the 7 lessons into my daily life. Following each story excerpt is a spiritual discourse on the lesson itself, including the wisdom gathered from many spiritual traditions and the potential pitfalls that can occur on this path. Also each chapter includes a section on **Transforming Your Life** that focuses on how this lesson might benefit you right now as you face the challenges of living on a disrupted planet Earth.

The Journey from Ego to Soul is actually a sequel to the book *7 Lessons for Living from the Dying*, which introduced the 7 lessons I learned from my hospice patients and their loved ones. If you haven't read *7 Lessons* you might benefit from doing that before you start this one. But it isn't absolutely necessary as this book can stand alone as well.

Each chapter of the book ends with a section of recommended **Tools for the Journey** to help you go deeper into the 7 lessons if you are interested in doing this work. There are also additional **Resources** for each chapter that you can find online by going to www.eoluniversity.com/resources.

The chapters are designed to be read in consecutive order because each lesson builds upon the previous lesson. However you are, of course, free to do as you like and read them in any order. You might also want to read the entire story of the "little clinic," which has been separated into 8 parts, in one sitting. The story sections are all in *italics* so that should make them easier to locate. Please read and use these contents in any way that suits you!

This book lends itself well to reading in a small study group. You could meet on a regular basis and work together on each lesson by doing the assignments in the **Tools for the Journey** section and discussing your own personal insights and challenges. On the **Resources** page mentioned above you will find additional suggestions for studying and learning together.

No matter how you choose to read and use *The Journey from Ego to Soul* I hope that it benefits your own spiritual journey. And be sure to keep this book on your shelf as you will most likely want to read it again in the future. Remember:

> *Spiritual growth happens one step at a time, but transformation can take place in an instant.*

May you find whatever you need for your unique and fascinating path within these pages.

1. FALLING APART

"Don't hold together what must fall apart.
The familiar life crumbles so the new life can begin."

- BRYANT H. MCGILL

Sooner or later everything falls apart. It's a fact of life that relationships break up, jobs come to an end, buildings crumble, health declines, or a virus spreads around the world, disrupting daily life and the global economy. Even stars and galaxies, far removed from our ordinary lives, eventually burn out. This tendency toward disintegration is a problem for us because we go through life imagining that things will stay the same as they are (or perhaps get better in the future.) But we don't recognize that all around us everything is gradually falling apart and we are shocked and devastated when we must cope with unexpected loss and grief.

"Dad died today."

These three words spoken by my brother when he called to tell me of our father's suicide marked the very moment my own world fell apart. His death dismantled the spiritual belief system I had constructed throughout my life up to that point. The theory that love is the force that heals had inspired my choice to enter medicine and supported me through my years of training. But Dad's suicide shattered that theory. All of my work to become a doctor who channels love to patients was suddenly made meaningless. What good was the love I channeled if it couldn't save one of the people I loved most in the world?

But this falling apart was actually an opening for a profound healing process that would change my life forever. I was about to embark on an experience that would unravel my ego and its attachments to how life "should" be so that I could become who I was always meant to be: my True Self.

When such tragedy strikes we are left with a choice: we can run *away* from the pain and bury our feelings or we can go *toward* the pain and allow ourselves to be broken open.

The path of brokenness leads ultimately to the opportunity for transformation and growth, which I later discovered. But gaining such wisdom requires each of us to take a journey in which we confront our own shortcomings, see the flaws in our beliefs, and recognize our limitations while we learn to genuinely love who we are and the life we have been given.

This journey takes us outside the ordinary experiences of daily life into a place where transformation and healing are possible. Through this inward journey we can become our True Selves, guided by the wisdom from our own Souls.

Throughout my own journey I discovered that guidance awaited me at every turn and "little miracles" occurred just when I needed them to help me keep learning and growing with each step. This book is the story of that inward journey and how my internal operating system shifted over time to become Soul-guided rather than ego-driven.

THE LITTLE TWO-ROOM SHELTER CLINIC

During my fourth year of medical practice, when I was a young doctor and a wife and mother with two tiny children, my father took his own life, which shattered my world and changed the trajectory of my life path forever. The grief and guilt I carried from his death were so immense that they ultimately crushed me. Where I had once been confident in my knowledge of life and love and how things work here on planet Earth, I became utterly fragmented—broken to bits by pain, grief and loss.

For the next three years I wandered through each day, dragging my heart behind me, just trying to hold all the pieces together. I felt confused and disillusioned—how could such senseless tragedy have any meaning at all? How could I incorporate Dad's violent death into the beautiful tapestry of my life, which was now torn to shreds? I had no idea how I would ever heal from this tragic devastation.

One day a favorite patient of mine, William, who came in frequently to have his heart condition monitored, confided in me that he had been having thoughts of suicide. He was the very same age my father was when he died by suicide. I was overcome with emotion to hear William talk about also wanting to end his life. Tearful and shaking I excused myself from the room while I tried to regain control and put on a more professional demeanor. But my thoughts were swirling with self-doubt and negativity: "I couldn't stop my father from killing himself. I'm not good enough to help William. I can't do this."

When I re-entered the exam room William immediately responded with concern for me, wondering why I had been so upset by his words. I told him about my father's suicide and apologized for not being in control of my emotions.

William was silent for a moment and then said, "I can see the great pain you are in. Until now I hadn't even thought about what taking my own life might do to my children but I needed to be reminded of that. I can't cause that kind of pain—the pain I see on your face—to the people I love. I won't do it—I will find a way to get through this."

That experience with William revealed to me just how much I was still affected by my unhealed grief. I worried that my pain was making it impossible for me to be a good doctor even though William had actually been helped by seeing my brokenness. I didn't know if I should continue to practice medicine. I couldn't see any way out of the dark tunnel where I was trapped.

Then one day I received an inspiration, which would turn out to be my first opportunity to step into what I would later come to call my inward journey. On that day I heard in my mind a directive to "Call hospice," even though I wasn't actually sure what a hospice did or if there was one in our community. But I listened to the message and I called a non-profit hospice in the area.

When I asked if there was any volunteer work I could do for them as a doctor, the woman on the other end of the line was speechless for a moment, then responded "Why did you decide to call us right now?"

"I don't know," I answered truthfully.

She went on to say that their medical director had just resigned earlier that day and they had been in a panic because they were legally unable to function without a doctor on staff. After declaring that my phone call was a "miracle" she invited me to be their new medical director even though I knew nothing about caring for dying patients. And so, just like that, I followed my intuition and received the opportunity to step onto a new path that eventually led me to become a full-time hospice medical director.

Visiting hospice patients was something I could do at that time in my life. I could bring all the broken pieces of my heart and shredded remnants of my belief system to the bedside of the dying and listen to their stories. I could spend hours with them, delving into their pain as I explored my own; searching with them for meaning in the midst of life's madness; and finding again the thread of love that had disappeared from my view several years before. Through that work I began examining death and loss and grief as they unfolded in the lives of our patients. I created my own "independent study course" in suffering, in hopes that I could eventually apply what I was learning to my own life and rise above grief to find joy again.

But it turned out that exploring death and dying through hospice work was not the only curriculum on my inward journey at that time. Shortly after I started working full-time in hospice I was introduced to a shelter in my community that housed women and children who were victims of domestic violence. Many of the residents had been brought to the shelter by police officers after being rescued from horrendous situations of physical and psychological abuse. The director of the facility gave me a tour and told me her dream was to start a small medical clinic within the shelter so that residents would not have to leave its safety to receive the healthcare they needed. In that moment, just as when I had heard the directive to call hospice, I felt a strong pull to help her create that little clinic, even though I was already quite busy as a hospice doctor. So on a whim that day, without really thinking about the commitment I was making, I volunteered to spend every Wednesday afternoon providing medical care to the residents of the shelter.

A few weeks later, as we were making plans for the clinic and how it might function within the shelter, the director delivered some potentially discouraging news: "We have only been able to set aside $200 in the budget for this clinic."

Not one to be easily defeated I responded, "Well we can work with that—$200 per month isn't much but we'll find a way to get by."

She paused and cleared her throat, then clarified her statement: "No … we have only $200 for an entire year!"

But even this news didn't deter me. For some reason I was determined to create this clinic and I decided in that moment that we would do it even without funding. I knew there had to be a way to make this happen, so I sent word out to my medical colleagues in the community, letting them know about our plans for the little clinic and asking for any equipment or supplies they would be willing to donate.

Over the next few weeks, donations began pouring into the shelter. One day we received a tattered exam table from a doctor who had recently upgraded the furnishings in his office. He apologized for its worn condition, but to us that table was beautiful, especially after we used duct tape in a matching color to patch up the torn upholstery. We also received a stethoscope, blood pressure cuff, oto-ophthalmoscope (for examining ears and eyes), glass apothecary jars, boxes of tongue depressors, cotton swabs, gauze and other bandaging supplies, medication samples, a microscope, and even an old, but still-functioning, EKG machine.

In addition to those donations, I was able to convince our local hospital to do laboratory testing for us free of charge. They provided us with culture tubes, microscope slides and the supplies for drawing blood. I also arranged with my husband's medical clinic to do occasional X-rays for our patients at no cost. Thanks to the amazing generosity of our medical community we were able to fully furnish that little shelter clinic within a few weeks.

Our physical space consisted of two rooms: one for patient intake—our "Office"—with a desk, several chairs and a filing cabinet; and the "Exam Room" with the patched up table and two chairs. The Exam Room also housed a tiny "Laboratory" on one end of the counter, a cabinet full of bandages and casting supplies, and a closet, which served as our "Pharmacy," filled with donated medication samples. Just like that, with no expense whatsoever, we had a *reasonably stocked, two-room clinic and were ready to start seeing patients.*

The fact that we were able to easily gather everything we needed for the clinic seems miraculous as I look back to those days. But now I also see it as validation that this was work I was meant to do as part of my inward journey. I had volunteered to start the clinic without having any idea what was in store for me, just as I had started my work at the local hospice without knowing why I had been inspired to be there. The little shelter clinic was going to become my laboratory where I could test and learn to embody the 7 lessons from the dying. These lessons were the stepping stones of a path laid out before me —a path that led me back toward wholeness, understanding and greater depth than I had ever realized before. Gradually my grief was being transformed into wisdom on this path of pain. These 7 lessons would change the way I saw everything. And my work in the little clinic would teach me to live in a way I had never before experienced: by the wise guidance of my Soul rather than the foolish inconsistencies of my ego.

As described in this story, the stage for an inward journey is often set before we even realize what is happening. We may find ourselves on a particular path and not recognize that we have been learning spiritual lessons all along until we can look back from a future time. How do we prepare for a journey if we don't know where we are going or when we will get there? That is what life asks of us when we set out to grow spiritually, whether we have started the journey willingly or been thrust onto the path by a sudden, unexpected crisis.

Steve Jobs, co-founder and CEO of Apple Inc., undertook his own inward journey when he was diagnosed with terminal

pancreatic cancer. He spoke these words during a commence-
ment address at Stanford in 2005:

---

*You can't connect the dots looking forward; you can
only connect them looking backwards. So you have to
trust that the dots will somehow connect in your future.
You have to trust in something – your gut, destiny, life,
karma, whatever.*

STEVE JOBS

Looking back I can see now, just as Steve Jobs described, that
trust was essential in my own inward journey: trust that I should
call hospice and become a volunteer and trust that I should start
a free clinic at the shelter with minimal resources available. The
growth I experienced on that path would not have been possible
without my ability to trust—that there is goodness in this
Universe, that love will prevail in the end, that no matter how
dark the hole into which we have fallen, there will always be
enough light to illuminate it when the time is right. Trust
enabled me to say "yes" and take the risks that changed everything for me.

As you read this book you will be asked to trust, as well. You
will need to go forward without answers or assurances that you
are on the right path. The strategy behind *The Journey from Ego
to Soul,* which is intended to be a guidebook for this travel into
the unknown, is to teach you about the landmarks encountered
along the way and the hazards you may experience as you travel

through life. Before you delve into the 7 lessons of this path you will need some tools to help you and this chapter will introduce you to the mindset and concepts necessary for navigating the inward journey. You will learn about Ego and Soul, the Garden and the Galaxy, The Dance of Life, Detours, Travel Advisories, and Rules of the Road—all to serve you on the journey ahead. Remember to keep trusting as you read on!

FROM EGO TO SOUL

This inward journey that I have been describing begins with the ego or lower self in charge of life's decisions and takes us eventually to the True Self or Soul providing guidance for life after the awakening and training of the ego. But what does this mean and why does it matter? You'll be learning all about ego and Soul in each subsequent chapter of the book but for now here are some basic definitions:

We humans primarily operate in the world through the functioning of our bodies, minds and our egos, which together can be referred to loosely as *lower self* or just *body/mind/ego*. According to Webster's Dictionary the ego "serves as the organized conscious mediator between the person and reality especially by functioning both in the perception of and adaptation to reality." Simply stated, the ego is the filter through which we view the world—like a window or a lens—and if the ego is damaged or distorted or cloudy, our perception of life will be distorted as well. The ego interprets what happens in the world and helps us decide how to react to the events around us. The ego also carries the awareness of being a unique individual or *separate self*—different and distinct from all others. But the wounds that have afflicted the lower self during development also have an influence. The ego protects these wounds, and the dysfunctional behaviors they trigger, within the Shadow where we are unable to see them in daily life. Our wounds help create the distortion and cloudiness that prevent the ego from accurately perceiving the world.

The Soul, on the other hand, is the part of us that always watches, always listens and has always known what is going on. The Soul is the *witness* of every aspect of our existence: every thought, every action, and every subconscious motivation or wound. Most of us are unaware of the presence of the Soul in our day-to-day activities but the Soul is totally aware of us at all times. Until we have an opportunity to undertake an inward journey, we relate to the world through the ego while the Soul remains a hidden and unheard watcher, whose wisdom and presence is generally ignored.

In spiritual terms, the Soul is also our direct connection to the Divine, to God, to the Source of Creation. The Soul or *higher self* is the repository of our highest potential, our greatest wisdom, and our purest creative energy. The Soul is the manifestation of *fearless love*, the point at which Spirit first takes on material form, the vortex at which Heaven becomes Earth. If this makes no sense to you right now, you will have to trust me. Keep reading even though you're not sure.

Because, what your ego cannot comprehend, your Soul *knows*. And your Soul is just waiting for the ego to allow it to begin influencing your life. Give my words and these stories a chance to connect with your silent Soul and watch for signs to appear that you have more wisdom and creativity and potential than you have ever imagined. Trust that the Soul knows exactly what you need in your life right now and gradually begin to change your relationship with your own Soul. That is part of the purpose of this book and the reason why the inward journey is important.

TAMING THE TIGER

As we examine the relationship between your ego and your Soul or True Self it is important to recognize that both aspects of your being are essential for your life here on planet Earth. Some spiritual teachings have labeled the ego as an "enemy" that must be overcome and vanquished, but in reality the ego is a vital ally for the Soul that requires training in order to carry out this role. Here is a story to help illustrate this relationship:

While doing research for another book I recently came across the legend of Durga who is an ancient warrior goddess in Hindu lore. As I understand it from my limited reading, Durga's role is to defeat evil and empower creativity for the sake of peace and the good of all existence. As a warrior goddess she is fierce when necessary but compassionate at the same time. She rides a tiger (or a lion in some myths) for transportation and has many arms that carry multiple weapons of destruction. She also carries a lotus blossom in one hand, a symbol for growth and birth. Durga relies on her well-trained tiger to help her move through the world and carry out her important work.

When I read the description of Durga riding her tiger while slaying demons and protecting all that is good, I was reminded of the relationship between the ego and the Soul. Durga represents the Soul, which has tools to overcome evil and foster creativity with great compassion, but also with fierceness. The tiger represents the ego, which is capable of doing great damage on its own but, when properly tamed, provides a vehicle for the Soul to operate in the world. This metaphor eventually became an important teacher for my own process of spiritual growth.

In the past I had feared the destructive tendency of my own ego as if it were a vicious, wild tiger and I attempted to control it by locking it away in a "cage" of repression so I could feel safe. But, just as Durga tames the tiger to become an essential companion for her work, I realized that I needed to utilize my Soul or Higher Wisdom to train my ego so that it could become (along with my mind and body) a vehicle for the creativity of my Soul.

This revelation helped me envision a new role for my primitive ego and forge a new collaboration between my "lower self" and my "higher self" or Soul. It became clear to me that disempowering my ego in the past had made it nearly impossible for me to step up and become a fierce protector of the good. While I had the Soul inclination to always live and create from love, I didn't have enough courage or "warrior strength" to do battle when necessary. I had difficulty speaking up and making my voice of wisdom heard because I didn't have enough "tiger" force to support me and carry me into challenging situations. So part of my homework on my inward journey was to release my ego from its cage and then teach it to surrender to the guidance of my Soul, without weakening its power to stand up for what is good. Like Durga I needed my ego/body/mind as a vehicle for my work: slaying the dragon of my fear, surviving the ordeal of my father's suicide, rediscovering the power of love, and ultimately transforming into my whole, True Self.

When I read a little more of Durga's story I was delighted to see that even the roots of her name are fitting for this metaphor I have adopted: *dur*, meaning difficult, and *gam*, which means to pass through. So Durga, for me, is the goddess who represents the ability to "pass through difficulty" or in other words, complete an inward journey by "taming the tiger" of lower self and living a life that is Soul-directed rather than ego-driven.

THE GARDEN AND THE GALAXY

In the book 7 *Lessons for Living from the Dying* I described two different perspectives on the events of life: the View from the

Garden, which is the outlook of the *lower self,* and the View from the Galaxy, which is the vantage point of the Soul. These two perspectives are important to keep in mind as we begin the journey described in this book as well.

The Garden is where our day-to-day lives unfold and where the ego exerts maximum influence. The Garden consists of our work, relationships, and general activities and is plagued by difficulties over which we have no control. Just as storms, drought, pestilence, and weeds may threaten the survival of an actual garden, our lives here on Earth face constant challenges from illness, loss, failure, disappointment and betrayal. Even the global pandemics that have threatened the entire world are part of the perilous functioning of the Garden. Working and surviving in this Garden of life requires ongoing attention to ever-changing details and can often be discouraging.

The Garden of life is governed primarily by two forces: *fear* and *greed.* The ego is particularly good at disguising both fear and greed so their presence may not always be obvious. But these are the secret tools of the egoic lower self that are designed to control behavior and outward appearances.

From a less personal perspective, fear and greed are also the forces that govern many systems that exist in our society. The stock market and financial industry are driven by both greed for greater profits and fear of financial losses. The insurance and healthcare systems rely on fear of future illness or injury to market their services. Politicians play on the fear and greed of their donors and constituents to get reelected, often stoking fears of harm from "other" groups of people. Businesses in all areas use the fear of not being good enough as a ploy to sell their products to insecure consumers.

Fear and greed are visible everywhere in the world as tools because most of us operate primarily through our egos and are susceptible to these forces. The most vile and destructive aspects of our society—racism, corruption, exploitation, brutality—arise from egos that are out of control and ungoverned by higher consciousness.

However, while the ego allows us to be both targets for external manipulation or predators toward others, it also plays a role in our survival. One of the functions of ego is to protect the Shadow aspect of the self: to hide away all of the dark deeds, deep wounds and ugly intentions that fester in the subconscious. The ego uses "smoke and mirrors" to cover up the dark parts of the self that are too frightening, painful or even too dangerous to perceive, particularly when we are not strong enough to confront our own darkness. But one of the great tasks of the spiritual journey is to gradually open the dark "cave" of the Shadow and shine light within so that the healing of past wounds can take place. Think of this as the process of letting the tiger out of its cage so that it can be tamed and empowered to act for the good.

While the fear and greed of the ego can be sources of destruction when they run wild in our lives, even they ultimately serve a positive purpose, because both of them arise from the instinct to survive. They are basic, primal functions of the self that ensure that our life on Earth can continue: *fear* helps protect us from danger while *greed* enables us to get what we need to stay alive. Chaos ensues only when fear and greed are not recognized or managed properly by the *lower self* as tools of growth and survival. Thus one of the important tasks of the *lower self* in the Garden is to gain control over these two instinctive drives.

The Garden can be a place of great pleasure, especially when things are going well and threats are minimal. Then there is ample time to notice the beauty that exists all around, the sensuality and abundance of life, and the satisfaction that arises from productivity. During these occasions we can rejoice in gratitude for all our blessings and be relatively unaware of greed and fear lurking in the background.

But when the Garden is under threat—the rain doesn't come, hail beats down, a virus runs rampant, or the ground isn't fertile—in other words, when life doesn't go the way we've hoped and expected, then fear and greed can show themselves to be ugly and cruel masters. Then our confidence breaks down and we discover that our current guidebook to life doesn't have a chapter on how to handle such disaster. We have no strategy for coping with illness, unemployment, loss and betrayal even though life in the Garden is filled with these difficulties.

The ego on its own runs out of options when confronted with devastation and can quickly sink into despair. But this falling apart—even when it affects the entire planet, such as climate change or a global pandemic—also provides an opportunity to wake up to the presence of higher consciousness, the Soul.

The **Galaxy View** is what is needed during times of distress to provide a bigger picture and a balanced perspective to the tragedies of the Garden. For the Galaxy view allows us to look at all of the events of life here in the Garden of Earth as if we were capable of seeing the entire Universe at once. From that lofty point of view, each disastrous event in the Garden is quite small compared to the immensity of the Cosmos, including global events like a pandemic. And it becomes apparent from the Galaxy view that there are more significant forces in motion than the greed and fear that govern the Garden.

The Galaxy view enables us to transcend the stresses of the Garden but does not exclude the necessary components of the Garden. This is an important point: spiritual growth doesn't mean that we eliminate the emotions and knowledge we acquired at an earlier time in our lives. We simply view them from a different perspective and act on them differently as we wake up and grow to higher consciousness.

So, greed and fear still exist at the Galaxy level, but they have grown into their noblest aspects as they support the highest good for all. For example, when *greed* appears at the Galaxy level it has been transformed into a drive to move forward, to evolve, and to manifest everything that is possible. And the *fear* that had the potential to be destructive within the Garden changes into an impetus to expose the Shadow and illuminate the forces of darkness when it exists at the Galaxy level.

From the Galaxy perspective we can recognize that we are connected to all of life and all of Spirit and that there is Divine momentum behind every event. There is no need for Garden-level *fear* because everything that happens from the Galaxy point-of-view is part of a continuum of growth and development. And the lowest forms of *greed* are not supported at the Galaxy level because what is needed has already been provided, as will be demonstrated when we look more deeply into the 7 lessons.

The equanimity of the Galaxy view offers the perfect counterbalance to the anxiety of the Garden, and both perspectives are necessary in order to survive on Earth, just as the goddess Durga needs her tiger to help her carry out her *fearless love*. The two views cannot be separated even though most of us live without awareness of the Galaxy, with no higher concept of life and its difficulties. The Galaxy view can only be attained by working toward more evolved consciousness, by undertaking an inward journey and empowering the Soul to connect us with this greater wisdom.

"GARDEN" KNOWLEDGE

The Garden where we conduct our day-to-day lives offers a great many learning experiences to help us expand our fund of knowledge throughout this lifetime. We learn through study, observation and participation in the events of life and we have the potential to become experts and authorities in many different areas if we apply ourselves to this task of acquiring knowledge. Life in this Garden is also dualistic, meaning everything has an opposite: light and dark, good and bad, right and wrong. Growth and creativity arise from the tension exerted between these polar opposites here in the Garden, so duality is necessary for life to exist, even though it leads to some difficulties for us.

In societies there is a tendency for people to separate into opposite sides over nearly every issue that affects us. From this polarity we can ideally find our way to a creative balance in the middle that provides the best compromise for everyone concerned. But again, these opposing views can be manipulated by external forces, using fear and greed, to divide us against one another. Then rather than focus on growth and wellbeing for all, we resort to undermining and destroying the other side, which ultimately weakens and depletes society as a whole. Again this risk arises from the natural duality of lower consciousness and can only be transcended by waking up and growing spiritually.

This duality applies, as well, to the thought processes and the modes of action that occur at lower levels of consciousness within the Garden. From a simplified perspective the two opposing ways of thinking and acting at the Garden level are *linear* and *circular*. *Linear thinking* tends to be more masculine in its type and exemplifies much of Western thought; while *circular thinking* is more feminine and commonly influences

Eastern thought. Note that each person possess both masculine and feminine aspects, so these ways of thinking apply to everyone, and are not specific to gender.

Linear thinking is oriented toward forward motion, moving ahead along a straight line, while leaving behind everything of the past. This linear pattern of thought and action is good for getting things done and pushing on through difficulties. Linear thought is goal-oriented and can lead to progress, however it poses some problems, as well. Because the linear thinking process tends to ignore the past, a linear mind struggles to learn from previous experiences. Thus some failures may have to be repeated multiple times before a linear thinker can recognize the danger there and avoid making the same mistakes again. Linear thinking at its worst can lead to behavior motivated solely by greed while ignoring the consequences of these actions.

Circular thinking, in contrast, recognizes and values that all things are connected and that the past, present and future ultimately flow together in one continuous cycle. This pattern of thought is very respectful of lessons learned in the past and honors that acquired knowledge in current decisions. The danger of circular thinking, however, is that when fear is present no progress can be made. Thoughts and actions can get stuck in a constantly turning circle that cannot escape from the burdens of the past or move forward. Circular thinking can then lead to a lack of action because of too much weight from the past.

So both ways of thought and action, linear and circular, have their limitations here in the Garden where we live out our daily lives. These thought patterns can lead to some of our common problems: such as destroying the environment because we cannot perceive that we are connected to nature and that our own survival depends on the health of the planet; or becoming trapped in a cycle of war as an expression of power because it is instinctual to us and we cannot see a way to move forward without it; or denying the potential threat of a rampant viral infection in our community because it doesn't fit with our current worldview. Other negative expressions of linear or circular patterns of thinking include adhering to rigid ideologies from the past rather than allowing our beliefs and guiding wisdom to evolve over time; or obsessing over the superficialities of life, such as material possessions, wealth and success, because in our search for pleasure we cannot perceive the deeper meaning of genuine joy.

THE SPIRAL OF THE GALAXY

"Do not look back,
no one knows how the world ever began.
Do not fear the future, nothing lasts forever.
If you dwell on the past or future, you will miss the
*   moment."*

-RUMI

The duality of the Garden can be discouraging, however from the Galaxy perspective it is possible to transcend both the rush toward the future of linear thinking and the stagnation in the past of circular thinking. To begin with, at this Galaxy level the emphasis is on *being* rather than thinking or doing. *Being* takes place only in the present moment so it does not propel us toward the past or the future, it simply allows us to balance in the here and now. In addition, this *being* of the Galaxy level also includes and embraces every aspect of the Garden level even while it transcends and expands upon the Garden. Confusing, yes?

Here's another way of explaining the Galaxy view: it includes both patterns of thinking that are seen at the Garden level of thought, linear and circular. Therefore the Galaxy perspective of *being* is continuously moving in a forward direction (like linear thought) because it is new in each and every moment; and the Galaxy perspective also circles around again and again (like circular thinking), leaving nothing out. In other words, from the Galaxy view, growth occurs in the pattern of an ever-expanding *spiral*, the perfect combination of a line and a circle. So this spiral motion at the Galaxy level allows for continuous progress (even though it might be very small) and continuous revision of the past to create ever-expanding *wisdom*.

This Galaxy way of *being* is where genuine wisdom is generated – wisdom that can inform our decisions and actions, guide us to the best choices for the greatest good for all, inspire us toward higher qualities such as compassion, courage, integrity and *fearless love*. Tapping into this wisdom is the greatest gift the Soul has to offer, even though wisdom alone is not enough for survival on this planet. Ultimately the knowledge of the Garden gained by the lower self is also crucial for our existence here, just as Durga needs the power of the tiger in order to move through the world. So the Garden and Galaxy are in balance with one another and the Soul needs the ego as much as the ego needs the Soul.

THE PARADOX OF THE SPIRITUAL JOURNEY

As you read the stories and lessons contained in this book it may seem that there are numerous contradictions in the messages that are being conveyed. We are alone on our journeys yet we are connected to everything and share our suffering with all of mankind. We have all of the answers we need within us yet we must cope with having no answers and no certainty about the direction of our lives. These seemingly opposite truths can be confusing and throw us off balance. But they arise from the two different perspectives we have been discussing, the views from the Garden and the Galaxy.

Your "Garden-view" of life is limited to the understanding of your mind and ego, which perceive you to be a solitary individual, separate from everyone and everything else. As you begin to grow in spiritual awareness you will gradually be able to view life from the Galaxy too. This expanded consciousness will reveal the interconnectedness of all things in the Universe, the higher purpose of existence, and the Divine energy that flows through all creation.

As you learn and grow you will become more adept at holding both of these views at once: "I am connected to everything but my mind/body/ego is a singular manifestation of the Divine here on Earth. I journey and grieve on my own unique path but everyone else is traveling a similar journey through life. I have everything I need within me at all times, but I can't see the answers clearly yet so I will just keep moving along my path." As a simple exercise to remind you to honor both perspectives, envision holding the Garden view in one hand and the Galaxy view in the other, then place your hands together over your heart. You are a spirit within a physical body, here to bring Heaven to Earth by holding both within your heart at all times.

2. WHEN EGO MEETS SOUL

"You think you belong to this world of dust and matter.
Out of this dust you have created a personal image, and
have forgotten about the essence of your true origin."

- RUMI

Activating the Soul is the key to maximizing potential during this life on Earth, in this Garden. When the Soul is operative it provides an ongoing view from the Galaxy to encourage and support the lower self. The Soul can assist the ego in decision-making, relationships, planning, and the healing of old wounds. But the Soul must be strong and functional in order to play this role. For most of us the gifts of the Soul have been locked away like gold coins hidden in an old trunk in the attic. Until they are found and put to use they have no value to us and we will never benefit from the fortune they can yield for our lives.

The problem lies in the fact that the ego is unaware of the

Soul and cannot perceive the presence of the Soul. In fact, the ego feels threatened by the very notion that a Soul exists and that it can provide direction and wisdom. This wariness of the ego is one of the greatest obstacles to activating and empowering the Soul, which is why even reading these words can create discomfort and resistance for some. But, once again, it is important to continue reading, even if doubt is rising within you in this moment. Keep moving forward and just take in this information without judging for now. If you feel negative and uncomfortable it is a sign that this is a discussion you need to hear, so don't give up just yet.

The ego rejects the idea of a Soul because it is trying to protect you from harm and embarrassment. The ego fears the unknown and will always choose what is visible and tangible over things that cannot be seen. This is a normal stage in the process of spiritual development and should not be viewed as discouraging. Simply go along with the flow of information and allow the negative thoughts to rise and fall.

The ego will resist the Soul until it is forced to give in, whether due to spiritual training that results in growing awareness or due to the humiliation and dismantling of the ego that occurs through the events of life. Ultimately, at the end of life, when the physical body and all its material concerns are fading away and when the ego is exhausted from trying to forestall its own demise, the Soul is finally able to shine forth in its radiant beauty. This illumination of the Soul was described over and over again in the stories of the hospice patients in 7 *Lessons for Living from the Dying*. Those stories taught us that the Soul will inevitably prevail over the lower self because the body, mind and ego will die in this physical realm, while the essence of the Soul will continue as it dissolves back into Spirit.

So why bother to activate the Soul now if it will eventually arise at the end of life anyway? Truly most of us live our entire lives without knowledge of the Soul—so what difference does it make? Why do this work now?

The answer is simple: because your Soul holds the key to your life purpose. Your Soul can enable you to have deep and rich relationships, help you manifest your highest potential and spark never-before-imagined creativity. Your Soul is exactly what you have been waiting for your entire life.

THE HOLE INSIDE

In all of my work in medicine over the years, whether in the primary care office, mental health center, hospice or homeless shelter, I have heard one consistent complaint from nearly every patient I have encountered (and from every colleague and staff member, as well): "I feel like there's a hole inside of me. Something is missing and I don't know what it is."

We are born into this physical realm with a deep longing for connectedness that we seek to fill with relationships, material possessions, food, drugs, sex, work, or pleasurable activities. But the connection we actually desire is to merge with the Divine and that desire cannot be satisfied with earthly or material attachments. The void we feel within us can only be filled by our own Soul, which is always already present, yet invisible to us.

We constantly seek pleasure as an antidote to the pain of this hole inside us. And pleasure does provide temporary relief, allowing us to forget that we have been hurting, that we have been searching forever for answers to our questions. But the gratification is short-lived and the reality of life's difficulties soon takes hold once more, compelling us to binge on pleasure all over again. We are actually longing for genuine *joy*, which comes from the Soul and is soothing and deeply satisfying. But because we are blind to the presence of the Soul and can't experience the joy it holds for us, we must instead settle for constantly feeding and tending our addiction to pleasure.

Marketers understand the desire for pleasure and the psychology of fear and greed quite well and utilize these emotions to relentlessly sell us products we don't really need. We receive a steady bombardment of messages that we are not good enough or don't own enough possessions through clever advertising that creates an insatiable desire for *more*: more stuff, more excitement, more education, more power, more money, more freedom, more pleasure. When we have an aching hole inside we can't refuse the opportunity to fill it with anything available so we are ripe for exploitation and manipulation by groups who want to sell their wares to us.

As a result we have become a society of over-consumption, driven by our emptiness to take in more and more pleasures in a futile attempt to fill up the hole inside. Fear and greed are the masters that control our gluttonous behavior and stuff us to the point where we suffer from obesity, both of the physical body and of the ego, as well. Even our corporations, financial institutions, political organizations, and healthcare companies are bloated and corrupt, serving primarily to feed themselves rather than to benefit mankind; and our religious establishments too have overindulged, with mega-churches, millionaire celebrity preachers, and bulging expense accounts. This over-consumption is destroying our health and killing our planet and it's time to stop.

There is no answer for this bottomless pit at the core of our existence except to discover the Soul—the part of us that is eternal and has always already been waiting to reveal to us that we are nothing more or less than the Divine taking on a physical form. If we do this work now we will have the opportunity to truly bring our gifts to the world and maximize their potential. And if enough of us take this journey we may have a chance to see life on this planet unfold and transcend the disasters that threaten its very existence. Isn't it worth it to join in this dance?

THE DANCE OF LIFE

> *"We are travelers on a cosmic journey, stardust, swirling and dancing in the eddies and whirlpools of infinity."*
>
> -PAULO COELHO, *THE ALCHEMIST*

Even though the Soul holds the secret to your creative potential and fulfillment of your purpose in this life, the Soul cannot function on Earth without the lower self. With no physical or egoic presence the Soul cannot act or create or discover or relate in the Garden of this world. For this reason, the Soul actually does not wrestle or wage war with the ego in order to gain control. The Soul recognizes that partnership and cooperation are essential for transcendence. So the Soul bides its time, patiently waiting in the wings, watching for the right opportunity to join the lower self in the dance of life. Together the self and the Soul can sway with the music of the planet, respond to changes in tempo and rhythm, and choreograph a life of beautiful movement. The Soul cannot step without the self and the self cannot hear the music without the Soul.

But to carry this metaphor further, the Soul does not force its way onto the dance floor—it must be invited or permitted to step into the movement already established by the lower self. That is why so many people on this planet are sleepwalking through life rather than dancing: their Souls have not been asked or allowed to participate. Unable to hear the music, the solitary ego creates clumsy choreography that is lacking in the core elements of dance: timing, balance, rhythm and grace.

These four elements were discussed in 7 *Lessons for Living from the Dying* and shown to be interwoven throughout the stories of the dying. First, the element of **timing** provides both *synchronicity*, when all forces align and work together, and *patience*, to allow events to unfold according to their own schedule, without rushing or forcing them to completion. **Balance** is the element that permits two partners to move together, each compensating for the rising and falling of the other by falling and rising, in turn. The **rhythm** of the dance is determined by the music of the Universe and gently pushes the flow of movement back and forth. Finally, **grace** is the limitless field of abundance that surrounds and inspires the dancers.

If only the ego could understand that what is missing inside is the music to inspire the dance and that the Soul is ready and waiting to provide access to the melodies of the Universe. To one who is awake and hears the music it seems so obvious, but to the ego that slumbers in the illusion of separateness, there is a vast wilderness between the two would-be partners, requiring a courageous journey of exploration before they can be united. And so the lower self that desires fulfillment must take on the challenge of this expedition to retrieve and unite with the Soul.

In this book, each of the lessons described in 7 *Lessons for Living from the Dying* will be presented again as a challenge that the traveler must face and overcome on the inward journey. In addition as part of this journey the spiritual explorer must allow the ego to be transformed by each lesson and be willing to emerge from the experience as an entirely new person. This need for transformation is the essence of the inward journey but also the greatest obstacle to its completion. Many of us prefer the comfort of sameness and resist the idea of change, therefore, in the end, we cannot agree to this process of spiritual growth. We might go through the motions or create the superficial illusion of transformation, but ultimately we hold tightly to our current reality and refuse to change. This form of "pseudo-spirituality" is a great trap created by the ego that has taken many spiritual seekers down a path that leads to nowhere. The intention of this book, once again, is to assist the reader on a personal journey toward spiritual growth and to serve as a travel guide that can point out such traps and dangers that may arise.

DETOURS ALONG THE ROAD

One of the important issues we must face on any journey is that the road is never as smooth or direct as we would like it to be. As we pursue our goal of spiritual growth we are likely to find many obstacles along the way, some that are specifically related to the lesson we are struggling to learn. Remember that even the detours that seem to take us far from our expected route are part of our learning process. We must strive to embrace the unexpected events and "road closures" that crop up on our journey, for they may lead us precisely to knowledge that will be necessary at a later time.

In fact, an unplanned "setback" may actually represent a great opportunity for an important course correction or for some remedial learning to take place:

Shortly after my first book was released I was involved in a cycling accident that resulted in a concussion and a broken collarbone. At that particular time I was in the middle of an exhausting marketing and promotion plan for the book that consumed every waking

moment of my time. But the accident left me unable to type, read, or even watch television for a few weeks. I was forced to simply sit and rest while my body recovered from these injuries. Initially I was in a state of panic because I wasn't able to fulfill any of my marketing goals and I missed some opportunities to promote the book that I thought were very important. I couldn't understand why this had happened to me at that particular time and lapsed into despair because my carefully designed plans had been ruined. However, during those weeks that I sat on my couch unable to do anything, I received an interview request from a USA Today reporter, which was totally unexpected, and a publisher in South Korea purchased the foreign rights to the book. So while I was being diverted off my carefully planned path to get the book out to the world, the important work was still taking place – without me!

This detour on my journey was a reminder to me that I needed to focus on **being** in addition to **doing** and that I am not really in control of things that happen *to* me or *for* me. I needed to correct my assumption that I could force my book into the world by sheer determination and learn, instead, to be patient and wait for the path to unfold in its own time.

Pay attention to the detours that occur along your own journey. In fact, when things seem to be going wrong, "look alive" for that is a sign that you are being redirected, that some surprising and important lesson may be on the way. Learn to revel in the uncertainty and welcome the unplanned—even when it is uncomfortable—for therein lies your opportunity for growth.

YOUR PERSONAL ITINERARY

"No one saves us but ourselves. No one can and no one may. We ourselves must walk the path."

- BUDDHA

To benefit most from this book it will be necessary for you to focus on your own personal experiences and the challenges that have brought you spiritual wisdom. Remember that reading about spiritual transformation is not the same as actually accomplishing the growth. You must be able to assess those areas in your life where you most need to grow and then create your own itinerary for your journey. You will have to become your own taskmaster and assign yourself certain practices, hold yourself accountable, and recognize when it is time to move on.

Ultimately spiritual growth occurs in ever-widening spirals as we continually circle around through the same lessons over and over again, making a little bit of progress each time.

Be patient and forgiving of yourself during this journey, but set a high standard of integrity and stay the course. After all an explorer on a great adventure cannot simply abandon the quest and give up, no matter how discouraging or difficult the task may be. Once you are on the path there is no turning back, so dig deep and keep moving, just a little each day.

Keep in mind that your life may have provided you with unexpected teachers along the way. Look back through your own history and make note of people who caused you distress or situations that pushed your limits. Those experiences may have been "lessons in disguise," there to expose a part of your Shadow or to reveal your hidden greatness. Encounters with teachers such as these are important markers of your journey up to this point so be open to remembering events that may have been painful for you at the time. A good explorer leaves no stone unturned and is willing to mine every rock pile for the gold it contains.

TRAVEL ADVISORY

For the purpose of this journey you must know who is in the driver's seat of your life: ego or Soul? According to Ram Dass: "The ego can masquerade as anything ... even Emptiness." In other words the ego is capable of imitating the Soul and creating a pseudo-spiritual experience that can mislead us. You must get to know the workings of your own ego so that you can differentiate it from Soul. Even many spiritual masters have admitted to being tricked by the ego at times during their development, so take this warning seriously.

Here are some characteristic behaviors of the ego to watch out for in general. The ego is likely to **measure, analyze, compare, criticize, judge,** and **argue.** Meanwhile, the Soul tends to be **accepting** and **tolerant**, even while holding firm to **values** and **principles**. The Soul craves **connection** and looks for areas of **agreement** while also maintaining **balance**.

The ego favors **rules, productivity, numbers, fairness,** and **doing**, while the Soul recognizes a **higher purpose, mystery, timelessness, emptiness** and **being.** The ego may spend a great deal of time in the past, trying to figure out who to blame when things have gone wrong, while the Soul sees that everything is perfect, just as it is. The ego also projects fear into the future, worrying incessantly over things that cannot be known, but the Soul is calmly unconcerned with what has not yet happened. The ego complains about how unfairly it has been treated while the Soul recognizes that life may appear to be unfair from the Garden perspective but things look entirely different from the Galaxy view, where the goal is to achieve the greatest good for *all*.

In the world currently as I write this book there are several authoritarian leaders in various countries who have been labeled as "narcissistic" and offer perfect examples of ego-driven behavior. You can study their character traits to better understand the worst aspects of the ego: distorting the truth, blaming others for their own failures, making enemies of anyone who disagrees, seeing the world only through the lens of their own concerns, and manipulating others through fear and greed. Use these figures as a "case study" to help you recognize the less than desirable behaviors of your own ego. These leaders create chaos, confusion and harm in the countries they govern and likewise your own life can be damaged by an ego that is out of control.

Your ego is the part of you that clashes with other egos, fears that you are not good enough, wants to be loved and accepted, complains about unfairness, worries about failure, feels like a victim, can't stand to lose a contest, doesn't like to share with others, and gets jealous when someone else succeeds. It is important to get as familiar as possible with this ego of yours:

what triggers it to react in fear, when does it seize control, who is viewed as a threat or as a target?

In terms of your spiritual growth, your ego may be relatively easy to recognize in the beginning because it will resist the spiritual principles you are learning. So your doubts, negative thoughts, procrastinations and sabotaging behaviors will be obvious signs of the ego at work. But be aware that at some point during the process of gradual spiritual awakening the ego begins to grasp the idea that this "soul-business" may have something to offer and may be worth going along with for a ride, which can actually represent a spiritual emergency situation.

THE EGO IN ACTION

It is possible for the ego to conclude that being spiritually aware makes you "better than" others who are not so enlightened. That's when things become tricky and confusing, for the ego can actually hijack the entire spiritual journey and take you down a dead-end path if you're not careful. The opportunity to feel superior to others is very appealing to the ego, and even more so when arrogance can be disguised as something positive and desirable, like enlightenment. If you take a look at many "spiritual" leaders you will find some who turn out to be just overhyped egos dressed in pious costumes.

I once observed a conversation between two devout spiritual seekers who were each pointing out that the other's behavior was purely ego-driven. Each man displayed an arrogant self-righteousness as he called out the other man for being deluded by his own ego and both of them showed pure disdain for the ego of the other. I was fascinated as I watched this back-and-forth display of one ego trying to appear more spiritually elevated than another. The truth is that only the ego has contempt for another ego and only the ego would work so diligently to prove its supremacy. Ultimately, each man was correct in identifying the disguised ego of the other. But both were in error by not recognizing that their own hidden egos were delighting in proving the failures of the other.

The Soul has compassion for the foolishness of the ego and no need to prove it wrong. The Soul simply shines its brilliant light and illuminates the ego so that its wounds can be exposed, thereby creating an opportunity for examination of the Shadow and the possibility of healing by offering love to the wounded self. But this exposure is deeply feared by the ego and can trigger a cascade of defensive behaviors and attacks that divert attention from the ego's vulnerability. When this happens, the ego recoils and contracts, while the heart and mind shut down. No new information is allowed in through the walls of defense and then "weapons" of blame and recrimination are fired at anyone in the vicinity. This cycle of exposure and defensiveness can recur over and over again throughout one's lifetime as the ego continues to run and hide from the shining light of the Soul. For some of us the ego must exhaust all of its resources and evasive tactics before it will be ready to surrender to the Soul's simple calm presence.

Sometimes devout faith in God can appear to be arising from the Soul when the ego is actually in control. In these instances a "believer" may adamantly declare their right to worship as they choose, while at the same time denying others the right to their own form of worship. Again the ego cares about its own agenda and disregards the needs of other people while the Soul is not threatened by those with different views of the world or of God. The Soul can co-exist peacefully with other humans because it comprehends and embraces the connectedness of all life forms. For the Soul, there is one Creator and one Creation—to hate or reject another for being different is unthinkable.

Another pitfall that has arisen in modern society is a confusion of the earthly goals of the ego with the spiritual tasks of the Soul. There is a movement now to equate material and financial success with spiritual growth and to imply that those who have attained their desires for wealth and "prosperity" are spiritually advanced because they have tapped into Divine guidance and abundance. There are self-proclaimed "gurus" of this new era who offer to show others how to achieve the same status and wealth if they become followers and pay enough money for the "teachings" they receive.

While financial and material success can certainly be part of the spiritual path, they are not the purpose of spiritual growth and do not represent validation of one's "superior" Soul wisdom. In fact, from reading this description the hallmarks of the ego should be obvious here: words like success, achievement, and attainment are favorites of the ego and material comforts are definitely preferred by the ego over the sometimes difficult circumstances of genuine spiritual growth. So beware of the teachers and guides that offer to show you the "easy path" to manifesting your desires and dreams: it is likely to be another "road to nowhere" that can distract you for many years.

SHADOW WORK

As we navigate this tricky journey of spiritual growth it will be necessary to dig deep and work intentionally on the Shadow aspect of ourselves—the hidden wounds that the ego strives to protect and conceal. Shadow issues can be difficult to detect and can lead us directly to the ego traps that will be mentioned in every chapter.

It is important to get familiar with your own Shadow tendencies and maintain constant vigilance in order to minimize the disruption they can cause. Focus on what triggers your emotions in relationships, work settings, and day-to-day situations. What causes you to overreact or lose control of your words and behavior? When are you likely to experience an embarrassing outburst or attack on another person? These behaviors are symptoms of Shadow wounds beneath the surface that must be explored before they can be healed.

As you grow in consciousness be aware that the Shadow also houses those parts of your former self that you have rejected because you no longer agree with them. For example when you "wake up" to the idea that racism is wrong, you will be offended by any racist thoughts or values that you may have held in the past and firmly disown them. However, if you push away that racist part of yourself because you now see it as wrong, you will relegate racism to your own Shadow, where it will be hidden from your view. The dangerous outcome of this denial of any and all racism within yourself is that you will also become blind to hidden racism within society. So learn to view your old negative thoughts and attitudes as parts of yourself that you continue to work on and transcend, but keep them always visible rather than hidden in the Shadow.

When you begin to work on your own Shadow, remember Durga, who represents the higher self, riding the tiger or the lower self. She has ten arms, each carrying a weapon or tool that she can use with *fearless love* to overcome evil in the world. Her spear pierces through superficial outer layers to reveal what lies beneath, while her sword separates right from wrong. She wields a thunderbolt that can spark powerful insights and an axe that can be used both to destroy what does not belong and to build something new with what remains.

Durga's powerful actions represent the 3 steps of Shadow work: **Recognize** the negative behavior that arises from the hidden recesses of your Shadow; **Recover** from the behavior by finding love and forgiveness for your wounded or rejected self; **Rise above** the Shadow by finding a new way to react when you are triggered. Like Durga, you will need to cultivate tools to help you reveal and gradually come to terms with your Shadow. For each of the 7 lessons that follow there are specific practices recommended to assist you with this task.

This deep work is essential for spiritual growth and the revelation of the True Self. However some religious and spiritual traditions have forgotten this necessary step and focus on outer growth without tending to the inner foundation. Thus from time to time we see teachers who espouse values of simplicity and humility while secretly amassing financial wealth, and gurus who claim enlightenment but sexually abuse their students behind closed doors. Be diligent with your own inner Shadow work but also remember Durga's tenth tool, the lotus blossom, which is a symbol for beautiful consciousness arising from the mud of unawareness. One day your True Self, like the lotus blossom, will open in the sunlight and shine forth in beauty as a result of the work you have done in the dark depths of the Shadow.

RULES OF THE ROAD

While you are traveling on this spiritual path there are a few rules you should observe to help you have a worthwhile experience:

1. **Stay alert**. Pay attention to what you are reading and thinking. Keep your thoughts focused on the task at hand as much as possible. If you are tired, take a rest. You cannot learn and grow if you are unable to focus on the information that is being presented to you. This journey requires your full

awareness so maintain your physical and emotional health.

2. **Slow down and study the terrain**.
   Remember the spiritual journey is a slow and deliberate process and there is nothing to be gained by attempting to speed it up or rush past the sights. Even though you may wish to reach your destination more quickly, as when you travel by airplane, the point of this expedition is to notice every detail of the scenery that surrounds you and the sound of each footstep along the trail. Give up the ego's desire for instant results and take the necessary time to enjoy the journey, one step at a time.

3. **Let the path unfold.** In reality this travel experience has a destination that is unknown to you so there are no particular milestones to measure and no stops where you have reserved a room in advance. You will have to learn to take each experience as it comes to you and do the best you can wherever you are, which is one of the most profound lessons of this spiritual journey.

4. **Watch for signs along the way.** As you make your way through all the dangerous passages and harrowing events of life, be on the lookout for signs, those little synchronicities that point you in the right direction. You not only have to pay attention to see them, but you also have to be open to the possibility that you will be given guidance at times during this process. Begin to notice this guidance when it comes to you and be grateful for the assistance.

PACKING FOR THE JOURNEY

At the end of each chapter in this book you will find a section called **Tools for the Journey** that will include **Mindset Shifts**, **Shadow Work**, **Practices** and **Action Steps** related to that particular lesson to facilitate your own journey. Recording your thoughts and reflections in a journal or note-book can be very helpful with this process so plan ahead and have the necessary materials available. You can utilize these tools right away as you work through each lesson of this journey, step-by-step, or you can come back at a later time when you feel ready to tackle the work that is required.

You will be reminded over and over again to "pack lightly" on this journey, for any excess baggage you are carrying will slow down your progress and interfere with your enjoyment of the moment. For that reason many of the tools offered to you will help you look at the past and heal your old wounds, since that is a crucial step in the process of spiritual growth. Be prepared to confront some discomfort from the past and take this opportunity to finally deal with those old issues. It may take quite a bit of time to go through all the lessons in this way, but the healing you experience will make it worthwhile.

Remember that the process of spiritual awakening can be slow and the journey long and arduous, with many detours and dead-end streets along the way. The ego is likely to be an unwilling passenger who tries to subvert the process at every turn and crossroad. But once you begin this trek you will be compelled to continue, no matter how many delays and misfor-tunes occur. You will wait for an eternity, if necessary, for the ego to pause during one breathtaking moment, see the lumines-cence of the Soul, hear the music of the Universe, and finally surrender to its rhythm. And occasionally while you are waiting, just when a feeling of hopelessness is threatening to settle in, there will be a brief encounter when you will receive a glimpse of enlightenment, a "mini-satori" that will reveal what is possible with awareness of the Divine. You will be provided with just enough inspiration for the journey to continue, so take a deep breath and carry on, trusting that you will have what you need along this path.

TOOLS FOR THE JOURNEY

MINDSET SHIFT

Albert Einstein wrote: "We cannot solve our problems with the same thinking we used when we created them." In other words we need to change how we see and think about our lives before we can move forward with new, healthier behaviors and practices. For each of the 7 lessons that follow you will be presented with questions to answer in a new way, from a new perspective. Write about these questions in your journal and address them every day until you can see a different or larger meaning of the words.

SHADOW WORK

One of the most important aspects of transformative work on yourself is to heal and reincorporate your own Shadow parts that have been rejected and left in the darkness. Throughout the 7 lessons you will be offered various journaling prompts to help you address your Shadow issues. The **3-2-1 Process** created by Ken Wilber[1] and the Integral Institute is a technique you can use with each lesson as you identify and reintegrate your Shadow wounds. You'll find a more detailed description on the **Resources** webpage at www.eoluniversity.com/resources.

1. Think of a person who recently triggered negative thoughts or emotions in you and recall the situation you were in at that time.
2. Imagine that you can **FACE** that person and keep them in your awareness.
3. Next **TALK** to the person about your feelings and experiences when you were triggered by them.
4. Finally **BE** the other person and imagine what they were feeling at the time of your encounter.

You can also use this **FACE-TALK-BE** sequence with situations, memories, or dreams that trigger your Shadow emotions. For example, I once had a dream that a stranger was chasing me and I was running away in terror. The next day I recreated the dream in my mind but instead of fleeing I turned around to **FACE** the stranger. Then I **TALK**ed to him and asked what he wanted and why he was chasing me. Finally I **BE**came him and saw that he was actually just trying to protect me and my fear dissolved away immediately. The "stranger" was a part of myself that I had rejected long ago but I was now able to embrace and accept as "me.'

Practice

For each of the 7 lessons specific practices will be recommended to help you learn and incorporate that lesson. I recommend that you try them at least once to see what you think. Ultimately you might want to choose a few of them to continue on a daily or weekly basis as you work on your own growth process. One simple practice that you can always use in any situation is **Deep Breathing.** This exercise will help you calm down your anxiety, become more focused and relaxed, and think more clearly when things are falling apart:

Begin by sitting or lying down in a comfortable position. Breathe in slowly through your nose for a count of six. Hold your breath for a count of six, then exhale slowly through your mouth for a count of eight. Repeat several times.

ACTION STEP

Do an **Ego Assessment** for yourself. Become familiar with the tactics and strategies of your own ego by journaling about them. When you experience a difficulty or conflict during the day, write about how your ego might have been involved in the situation and also note if you received any guidance or wisdom from your Higher Self. This will help you learn to distinguish between your own ego and Soul as you strengthen your awareness.

To truly embody these lessons and incorporate their wisdom into your life you will need to learn new patterns and change your behavior. The recommended action steps in each chapter are just a way to get started. You will need to develop your own creative applications of the spiritual lessons as you go. Start now by making a **Life Journey Map**:

Spend a few moments reflecting back on your life as a whole, from your birth (or even your conception) until this very moment. Take a large piece of paper and use colored crayons or markers to draw a map of your **Life Journey**. Show the major detours your life has taken, especially times of difficulty or challenge such as illness, death, relocation, unemployment, betrayal, loss, failure. You might draw them as ups and downs, obstacles, disruptions, tangles, or dead ends. Label each major event with words or drawings so you can easily identify them in the future. Be as creative or simple as you would like but make it your own, for it will play a role in each of the 7 lessons ahead.

3. THE FIRST LESSON: SUFFERING

"Don't turn away.
Keep your gaze on the bandaged place.
That's where the Light enters you."

- RUMI

Our journey begins with the lesson of Suffering, for that is the greatest challenge of our existence here on planet Earth: how do we manage the pain that comes to us when things begin to fall apart? We give a great deal of energy in our society to the avoidance of suffering, but ultimately suffering cannot be denied. Life in human form consists of unavoidable losses, failures, disappointments, illnesses, and tragedies all mixed in with the experience of joy, love and hope.

We cannot escape the pain of life because it is tied to the joy we seek. In fact, Rumi's quote reminds us that our wounds, our flaws and our weaknesses are actually the portals through which Divine Light and Love can enter to provide us with illumination. Thus we must learn to embrace our own suffering and the suffering of all life, keeping our gaze, always, on those light-filled openings so that we can see our way along this dark journey—a perfect introduction to the story that highlights the First Lesson:

THE BANDAGED PLACES

When I started working at the shelter clinic I expected to be doing basic primary care medicine: treating sore throats and high blood pressure, helping patients get access to medications they needed for chronic illnesses, reviewing blood sugar results for those with diabetes, and caring for occasional headaches and stomach pains. I had thought it would be a nice simple counterbalance for the emotional stress of working with dying patients and their families in hospice. But I soon discovered that I was not prepared for some of the more difficult patients that came to visit me in the little two-room shelter clinic on Wednesday afternoons.

One day, a few months after we started this free clinic, Charlotte, the retired nurse who had volunteered to help me each Wednesday, handed me the chart for a new patient she had just checked in, saying "This one's for you."

The name on the chart said only "Sabrina" and the reason for the visit was listed simply as "Suture removal." I was surprised that Charlotte was handing over the chart to me because normally she would be pressing me for permission to remove the sutures herself—a skill she had learned during her many years of work as an emergency room nurse. But Charlotte said nothing more and walked away.

I could tell immediately by the use of a first name only on her chart that this woman was being kept at the shelter in secrecy for her own safety. She had been given a fictitious identity and no one was told her real name to prevent word of her whereabouts from getting out into the general public. Usually this occurred when a woman was thought to be in considerable danger and she would be secretly transferred to a facility in a different state within a few days after her arrival. But Sabrina couldn't be transferred until her sutures had been removed which was the reason for her visit to the clinic that day.

I entered the exam room to see a woman in her early thirties, wearing only a cloth gown, sitting on the table with her head bent down toward the floor. When I moved closer I finally understood why Charlotte had deferred this case to me. Sabrina had a total of 36 lacerations covering her chest, arms, face, and breasts. Her boyfriend, in a fit of drunken rage, had attacked her with a box cutter and literally ripped her to pieces, narrowly missing any major blood vessels that could have caused her to bleed to death.

Each laceration had been stitched in the emergency room before Sabrina had arrived at the shelter, a repair job that had taken hours to complete. Now more than a week later it was time to remove the sutures so that she could be transported to a safer location. The police report attached to her chart indicated that her assailant was still at-large and could be searching for her in order to finish the job he had started.

The sight of Sabrina's wounds left me stunned. The damage that had been done to her physical body was appalling—I had never before seen such trauma inflicted on one human being at the hands of another. Even though I was accustomed to seeing the physical ravages of cancer during my work in hospice, something about Sabrina's case unnerved me and I stood there speechless. I reminded myself that I had been able to care for any wound I had seen in hospice, even the most horrific infected or necrotic tissue, without feeling repulsed or overwhelmed. But Sabrina's wounds were somehow different. Those lacerations had been inflicted in hatred and rage by a person who supposedly loved her. While I could easily handle the physical care Sabrina needed, I had no idea how to deal with the emotional trauma that accompanied these wounds.

I began removing the sutures from Sabrina's lacerations, one-by-one, saying a silent prayer for her as I cut through each stitch. But still I was speechless. I couldn't find any words that might comfort her. It occurs to me now that those physical wounds actually represented damage that had been done to Sabrina's soul. Her body language revealed a broken and humiliated woman with no positive life-force, no will to survive, no joy, no ability to cherish the moment.

Even my most physically tormented and exhausted hospice patients had been surrounded by people who loved them and were willing to care for them night and day. Those patients still seemed to radiate life-force energy and still managed to find some meaning in their illness. But for Sabrina that day in the clinic there was only hopelessness and despair. This was a type of soul-shattering suffering I had never encountered before.

As I finished removing the last piece of suture thread, I gently placed one finger under Sabrina's chin to lift her face. Finally finding my words as her eyes met mine I said, "This was not your fault. You didn't cause this to happen."

A single tear fell from her eye and rolled down her cheek as Sabrina whispered, "He said I deserved it. I talked back to him and I shouldn't have."

I tried to tell her that she was an innocent victim of her boyfriend's cruelty, but my words had nowhere to land. Sabrina disappeared again, staring at the floor, completely out-of-reach from my voice or my presence.

I never saw Sabrina again after that day and never heard what happened to her. Her vacant expression and the scars that covered her body haunted me, but I was even more disturbed by my own inability to help her—to make a difference.

Sabrina would not be the only patient to challenge me during those years as a volunteer at the shelter clinic. On many occasions I would feel a similar helplessness and lack of preparation for the suffering I witnessed. While hospice work was building my confidence for assisting dying patients, my shelter work was revealing to me that I had very little to offer to those living with trauma and emotional pain. I was learning a great deal about the different types of suffering we experience in life and could clearly see my limitations in coping with the pain of these patients at the shelter.

But in reality I also faced an obstacle that arose from deep within my own Shadow: not knowing how to carry my own pain over my father's suicide death, which had left me deeply traumatized. I was just beginning my own necessary spiritual work that would allow me to heal my buried emotions of grief and guilt.

One day in the clinic a few months later I was asked to see a 7-year old girl, Sherry, who had been brought to the shelter with her mother after a vicious attack by her father. Earlier that day when her parents were in the midst of a physical fight, Sherry had pushed herself between them, hoping to get her father to stop hitting her mother. Instead he kicked Sherry in the abdomen to get her out of his way.

Even though Sherry had been examined in the emergency room and was cleared of any serious internal injury, she had not stopped crying since her arrival at the shelter a few hours earlier. The staff at the shelter wanted me to decide if they should take her back to the ER for further examination.

Once again I felt totally helpless as I saw this tiny girl curled up on the exam table, sobbing inconsolably and holding her abdomen. When I tried to examine her she screamed even more loudly and pushed me away, making it impossible for me to find out what was wrong. Fighting with my own insecurity and fear I stood there for a moment, not knowing what to do or say, unnerved as I had been with Sabrina. I was on the verge of giving up and telling the staff to take Sherry back to the ER, but I remembered the lesson I had been learning from my hospice patients: "Embrace Your Difficulties."

I had just begun to understand that in life it is important not to run away from pain but to go toward it, in order to learn what pain has to teach us. In that moment the word "embrace" echoed in my mind and without hesitating I scooped Sherry up and held her little, shaking body next to my chest in a loving caress. I sat with her in my arms, rocking gently back-and-forth on the chair, holding her for as long as it took for her crying to subside. I hummed to her softly as if I was rocking my newborn baby to sleep and I didn't let go.

Eventually she stopped crying and I was able to examine her abdomen as I held her in my arms. I found nothing alarming and concluded that her cries were coming from her broken heart, her young shattered soul. She was responding to the pain of being betrayed by her father, the one man on the planet who should have done anything and everything to protect her.

Just as with Sabrina, I never found out what happened to Sherry after that visit. That was one of the most difficult aspects of working in the shelter clinic: connecting deeply with so many women and children and never seeing them again; always wondering if we had made a difference and helped them find a new path in life—or if we had just represented a blip in the road, a tiny piece of bright scenery on a long and dismal journey.

But Sherry's visit had a profound effect on me. A vague fear and sadness rose within me as I recalled the painful childhood stories I had heard from both of my parents, who had suffered through physical and emotional abuse in their own families. For the first time I was beginning to understand the damage that such violence can cause to a child—damage that might never be healed and could lead someone like my father to resort to suicide some day in the future.

I went home that day to write a poem inspired by Sherry's story called "Dancin' Shoes." I sobbed uncontrollably throughout the writing of that poem. Later each time I tried to read it aloud I fell apart and cried from my broken heart, my own shattered soul. I couldn't figure out why Sherry's story affected me so deeply and I felt embarrassed and confused each time I cried while reading the poem.

Though I didn't recognize it at that time, my own wound of grief was being slowly opened so it could finally heal. Unseen arms of Love were gently embracing me so that my fear could dissipate over time. But I could not yet admit that, like Sherry, I had been betrayed by my father whose suicide had destroyed my innocence and trust in the world. I wasn't ready to face the anger that I was hiding deep inside toward the one man I had expected to protect me from harm.

For months I continued to flounder in my work at the clinic, feeling that I didn't have the knowledge or skills to truly help the trau-matized women and children who came to me as patients. I wondered at first if some other doctor would be better suited to this work. But eventually I recognized that I had somehow been "chosen" to create this clinic, just as I had been called to become a hospice physician. So I stayed the course and continued on this part of my journey even though I couldn't see where it was taking me.

Several months later I was finishing up the last chart at the end of a clinic session, when I received a phone call from a friend who worked at a men's homeless shelter a few blocks away. He wondered if I would be willing to help one of their clients who was complaining of a "sore" on his leg. Their shelter didn't have the necessary medical supplies to take care of the man so I decided to see him, even though men were not allowed at our facility. I was alone in the office since Charlotte had already gone home for the day and I knew I could sneak him in through the back door for a quick visit without creating a disturbance for the rest of the shelter.

When he knocked on the door I opened it to find a short grey-haired man with a scraggly beard and twinkling eyes, wearing a long canvas duster over a ragged shirt and torn pants. Placing his back-pack on a chair he reached for my hand and introduced himself as "Ben." His friendly smile charmed me instantly even though it revealed large gaps where many of his front teeth were missing.

When Ben pulled up his pant leg to show me his "sore" I saw that he was suffering from skin ulcerations due to poor circulation. Several of the wounds along his lower leg appeared to be infected and were oozing with watery fluid, which was the reason he came in for help. Because of the swelling in his leg I was concerned that he needed more aggressive treatment than I could offer in the little shelter clinic.

I told Ben I thought he should go to an urgent care clinic or the emergency room, but he just smiled and said, "Oh no, that's not for me. If you can't help me here I'll just keep on doin' what I been doin'. I just came for a few bandages."

Reluctantly I decided to offer him the best care I could considering our little clinic's limited resources. With a basin of water and an antiseptic sponge I began to clean Ben's wounds. I removed the dead tissue and crust that had formed over them to reveal the pink, living tissue that was underneath. Ben sat patiently without saying a word while I scrubbed away at his leg, even though it must have been painful for him.

After the lesions were clean I bandaged them and gave him a bag of gauze and tape to take with him. He was very grateful for this, but I didn't feel satisfied. I tried once more to convince him to go somewhere else for additional care, but he just chuckled as he shook his head no.

I explained that he would need to keep his leg elevated as much as possible and asked him where he usually slept at night.

He said, "Oh I got me a bee-yoo-tee-ful spot under a tree down by the river. It's so nice…"

His voice trailed off as he smiled and looked out the window, imagining that special place of his. I pushed him to stay at the men's shelter instead so that he could sleep on a bed and be more comfortable, but once again he refused.

Still trying to do something more to help, I went to our supply closet and found a pillow and a blanket that had been donated to us a few weeks earlier. I handed them to Ben and explained that he could use those to prop his leg up at night, which would help with the swelling and eventually allow the ulcerations to heal.

He smiled at me once again, being utterly patient with me as he handed back the blanket and pillow.

"You are so kind, ma'am. I thank you, but I have no need for these. You save them for somebody else. I already have everything I need – it's just perfect! See this big coat? When it's warm outside I sleep on top of it and it's a soft, cozy bed. And when it's cold I sleep underneath it and stay warm as can be all night long. And my backpack here … well that's my pillow. And it will hold my leg up real good every night just like you said."

Again, just as had happened so many times before, I felt helpless in the face of a patient's suffering. I wanted desperately to fix the problem and make everything better, but he wouldn't allow me to do more for him. In frustration I said, "I'm just trying to help you!"

He touched my arm and replied, "Oh ma'am you've helped me a lot and I thank you. You gave me kindness … that's what folks need…" Flashing his charming, toothless smile he added with a wink, "… and some bandages every now and again."

I noticed how beautiful his eyes were, shining and twinkling with the light of contentment and pure joy, and I didn't know what else to say.

With that Ben picked up his backpack and the bag of gauze and just before disappearing out the back door turned to say, "It was just perfect, ma'am … exactly what I needed."

I stood there for a moment in amazement at what had just happened. I had again been confronted with my feelings of inadequacy at that clinic, believing I lacked the proper emotional and spiritual tools to help a patient who was suffering.

But Ben had swept away my insecurities with his down-to-earth reminder, "You gave me kindness … that's what folks need."

That message resonated through me and showed me a new way to view my work at the clinic. Perhaps the best I could do some days was to simply offer a bandage, a gentle touch and a kind heart. Perhaps I wasn't really being asked to do anything more than be courageous enough to embrace the pain, to keep 'gazing at the bandaged places' with unflinching love. Perhaps that was enough. Perhaps it was ... truly ... perfect, after all.

This story portrays the awakening of my ego to the reality of suffering in the world. While I had witnessed the suffering of the sick and dying through my hospice work and I had experienced my own suffering over my father's suicide, I had not yet been initiated into the realm of suffering caused by one human being acting against another. The little shelter clinic turned out to be the perfect stage for that initiation as there I was exposed to story after story of unimaginable abuse and neglect. My heart broke open repeatedly as I witnessed the pain of women and children whose lives had never known the light of love, and my ego was humiliated that I had nothing to offer them. Old fears of being inadequate began to arise and gave me the perfect opportunity to face them. I had developed pride in my skills as a doctor and believed that I could "fix" whatever was wrong with the patients I saw, or at least make them better. The suffering I witnessed at the shelter clinic thrust me into the harsh reality that I cannot control or change the course of life by exerting my ego or using my knowledge. This new awareness caused me to dig deep and humble myself so that I was ready to learn the next lesson on my journey when Ben arrived with a message of hope for me.

THE PATH OF SUFFERING

According to legend, Siddartha Gautama, who was born in Nepal around the year 563 BCE and would eventually become the Buddha, experienced his own awakening to suffering when he was a young man. As the son of a wealthy family, Siddartha grew up surrounded by luxury and comfort and had been sheltered from witnessing the pain of the outside world throughout his youth. While he had every material possession he desired, Siddartha recognized that something was missing when he reached young adulthood. Leaving the safety of his family's royal palace to explore new territory, Siddartha reportedly had three encounters on three separate days where he witnessed first a very elderly and debilitated man, then a person who was ill with a horrible disease, and finally a funeral procession bearing a corpse. He had been introduced for the first time in his life to the suffering of aging, illness and death. This awakening initiated him into the *inward journey* that would one day lead to his enlightenment.

This journey to spiritual growth begins, necessarily, with the lesson of suffering, just as occurred for Siddartha on his path. For it is our suffering that makes room for the Divine light and awakens us to the search for relief from our pain. Suffering precedes all other lessons because it is the fundamental task of human existence.

How well we learn to negotiate our difficulties determines the quality and depth of the remainder of the journey—and we will continue to be presented with opportunities to learn about suffering until we master the ability to face our troubles directly and willingly.

The challenge of suffering comes down to this: whether the

suffering is our own or that of humankind, we must learn to keep our gaze upon it and not turn away. This is one of the most difficult lessons of the journey and one that we will continue to spiral through for our entire earthly existence.

In 7 *Lessons for Living from the Dying* we saw that suffering is universal and shared by all of life, and yet suffering is also unique to each individual. Thus we can support each other in the experience of suffering, but can never compare or measure our own suffering against that of another. We must learn to share the suffering of the whole world and at the same time to bear our own individual pain all alone, recognizing that it is part of the gift of our lives. In the preceding story, I was struggling to learn that suffering comes in many different forms, and each experience with suffering requires its own unique coping skills. I was shown this over and over through my work in hospice and in the shelter clinic as I worked to broaden and deepen my own ability to face up to difficulty with *fearless love*.

THE WISDOM OF SUFFERING

Aeschylus, the Greek playwright who is often considered the father of tragedy, wrote, "Wisdom comes alone through suffering." This is a burdensome truth for us to accept: that part of our purpose here on this planet is to grow in wisdom, but we can only acquire the necessary wisdom by experiencing difficulties. So we can choose to willingly follow this road of suffering and embrace whatever perils come our way while we learn; or we can resist and rebel against the inevitable struggles of life, refusing to learn until we receive the ease and fairness to which we believe we are entitled. However, the more effort and time we expend on rejecting our own suffering, the less energy and opportunity we have for expanding in wisdom.

And this same lesson applies to our approach to the

suffering we witness around us. For we truly are not able to remove or erase the pain that others are experiencing. That was the lesson I struggled with in this story: I desired to take away the pain of Sabrina and Sherry and Ben, and in fact believed I was supposed to "fix" them and make everything better. I was frustrated and felt inadequate when there was nothing tangible I could do to help. In my hospice work I had grown accustomed to being able to alleviate pain and discomfort with medication, to calm fear and anxiety, and to help repair damaged relationships for my dying patients and their families. But in the shelter clinic I encountered a different type of suffering that challenged me greatly. There seemed to be no possibility of alleviating or repairing the pain I witnessed, and that situation left me feeling helpless.

Spiritual teacher Ram Dass points out in his book *How Can I Help?* that often the desire to help others comes with a hidden agenda, such as a need to cover up our own feelings of helplessness or to believe that we are "good enough" or to feel superior to the person being helped. All of these motives clearly come from the ego, which struggles to truly care for others and operates primarily from self-interest. The ego seeks to overcome the pain of others to prove that it is more powerful than any suffering that can occur, but this is a false goal that can never be attained. In reality, the ego is terrified of its own pain that cannot be controlled. In my case, I was still in pain over my father's death—a pain that no one could remove from me—and I sought to take away my patients' pain as a way of covering up my own need to heal.

But we are unable to eliminate our own suffering or that of others precisely because suffering is a necessary component of our individual paths. French novelist Marcel Proust wrote, "We are healed from suffering only by experiencing it to the full." Thus, even though it is a difficult reality to fathom, we are not granted the power to eliminate all suffering, either our own or that of another, because it is an important component of the path to wisdom. Of course we must help where we can and offer what we have to those who suffer, but we have to accept that there are limits to such "help." I had nothing to offer Sabrina because she was on her own road of suffering and had to find her own way to healing. And I needed to recognize my own suffering that was hiding underneath my fervent desire to help. When I held Sherry in my arms as a last resort, I finally listened to my higher guidance, which told me to simply "embrace" the suffering that was before me rather than trying to eliminate it, and that shift in mindset made all the difference.

Poet Kahlil Gibran wrote: "Out of suffering have emerged the strongest souls; the most massive characters are seared with scars," which means that to take away all suffering would also eliminate an opportunity to grow into a strong soul. This wisdom of suffering is not easy to grasp and can seem cruel and inhumane. But it is vitally important that we continue to look at it without turning away.

Gautama Buddha, who based his religious teachings on the alleviation of suffering, said: "Suffering, if it does not diminish love, will transport us to the furthest shore." He was saying, in agreement with Kahlil Gibran, that suffering itself holds the potential for our transformation, but—and this is important to recognize—it must "not diminish love." Love ... *fearless love* ... must be allowed a place in the midst of suffering if it is to become a catalyst for growth.

So spiritual evolution hinges on our ability to negotiate suffering—it cannot be skipped over or ignored—and love must be present within our suffering for that evolution to occur. That was the difference between the suffering I saw in hospice and the suffering of the women and children at the shelter. My hospice patients were generally surrounded by love as they moved through the last days of their lives, from family, friends and our staff. But the women and children at the shelter had ended up there because of an absence of love in their lives. That need for love in the midst of suffering was the most important lesson for me to grasp from my work at the shelter and one that I would continue to study every week.

The remaining six lessons I learned from my hospice patients can help us cope with pain and gradually redefine it, but we cannot travel through those lessons without first stepping onto and embracing the path of suffering. We live in a society that is addicted to positive thinking and the magical "law of attraction," which implies that we can create the life we want simply by thinking the right thoughts. There is some truth to this, because we must learn to harness and utilize the great capacity of our minds in order to complete our inward journey of spiritual growth. But the proponents of this "law" would have us believe that we can destroy suffering by denying it and refusing to see its existence. This is actually the very strategy that solidifies our pain and keeps us stuck there, all the while turning our focus in the wrong direction and propelling us down a dead-end road.

DETOURS ALONG THE ROAD

Such false promises of an easier life are one of the dangers we face on this journey. Why wouldn't we choose to be free of all negativity and suffering if that were possible? And the allure of acquiring anything and everything that we desire is so tantalizing that we will abandon our purpose and reason in order to follow the shiny path of materialism. But it is a blind alley that cannot take us where we need to go spiritually. When we stay on the difficult path that unfolds for us, even though we are suffering, we will ultimately find our way through and beyond the pain. And all of the riches we desire can still come to us on that path—they just may not arrive as easily as we had hoped or with the timing we would prefer. So we must do our best to stay on the "road less traveled" even with all the "scenic attractions" that slow down our progress.

Remember that detours are actually part of the journey and may be opportunities to discover a new path or to be nudged in a different direction. Detours on our road of spiritual growth are not negative or harmful experiences, though they do pose some threats to us: we must be cautious not to allow a detour to throw us completely off the path or cause us to become stuck in one place and unable to move forward. Then the detour becomes instead a dead-end and our growth can stagnate until we find our way back to the path. Be mindful when these detours appear in your life because they represent an opportunity for *fearless love* to enter and change everything. Keep in mind the Chinese character for *crisis*, which consists of two words: danger and opportunity. A crisis therefore is a *dangerous opportunity* for spiritual growth to occur.

Illness and injury are two of the physical challenges that can cause a detour along our path, though they are two of the most common sources of suffering in our lives. We can spend years wandering with our ailments through the vast wasteland of our medical system as we seek cures and healing that may or may not be possible. Meanwhile if we can wake up during this process we can actually keep learning and growing in wisdom even while we are pursuing various treatments for our sickness. When we remember that growth is the true purpose of the inward journey, then we can begin to recognize our progress, even if we remain physically ill.

One of the reasons that hospice patients seem to progress rapidly toward deeper spiritual understanding is the fact that they have exhausted all avenues for possible "cures" for their illnesses. Once they are freed from this search for a medical solution to the problem of mortality, they can turn all their attention and energy to the issues that "really matter" in life. They can keep their gaze on the "bandaged places" and truly bask in the light and love that enter there because they are no longer trying to eliminate the cause of their suffering, but instead are finding ways to embrace it.

Likewise, **failures and disappointments** can throw us off the path, even though they may represent course corrections that are actually diverting us toward a new direction we hadn't considered before. Problems occur if we get overwhelmed by failure and sink into a state of hopelessness, where we can stay trapped for a long time. Our underlying level of self-esteem determines how we view and respond to the detour of failure; so we may have to dig deep and undergo a great deal of inner healing work before we can rescue ourselves from such a trap. Ultimately, though, resilience is one of the qualities gained by learning this lesson of suffering, so failure becomes easier to negotiate over time and poses less threat to our forward progress on the journey.

Loss and grief are additional detours that can turn into dead ends as we travel this road. In my own case, I was mired in grief over my father's suicide death for many years, even though I was seeking to find my way out of that trap all along. But I had much to learn and needed to stay in that place of pain for a lengthy time so that I could experience every aspect of the "detour" of loss and grief. Going *through* the suffering, rather than trying to find a way around it, was the method that eventually brought me back to the light, though there were many years when I doubted that I would ever see that light again. The slender threads of hope I held onto in the midst of darkness ultimately led me out of it so that I could share the story and connect with the suffering of others, as well. This strong sense of connectedness is another gift that is bestowed by our journey of suffering and allows us to lessen the burdens of other travelers we meet along the way with our *fearless love*.

THE EGO AND SUFFERING

From the vantage point of the ego, suffering is a disaster that must be avoided at all costs. Difficulties are unwelcome and undeserved according to the ego, therefore it is imperative to determine who, or what, is to blame for things that have gone wrong. The ego feels insulted by the very idea that illness, failure and loss can occur and interfere with its plans and is threatened by the perceived loss of control over this existence. Furthermore the emotional tools needed for coping with difficulty may be limited, especially if the ego has been deeply wounded in the past and self-esteem is low. This was the case for many of the women and children I saw at the shelter clinic, like Sabrina, who had never had the opportunity to develop a healthy regard for herself.

During times of distress the lower self may react by withdrawing or shutting down, in order to avoid additional injury. This strategy leads to problems because it cuts off the flow of energy and prevents movement from occurring in any direction. Then it is possible to "get stuck" in the middle of the suffering until something else occurs to cause a shift. Energy is wasted even in the shutdown mode because there is a tendency to "spin the wheels" while making futile, weak attempts to get out of the trap. This mode of coping can occur when suffering diminishes love, which Gautama Buddha warned against.

For individuals who have developed stronger egos, the common reaction to difficulty is to find someone or something else to blame for everything that has happened, as mentioned above. In this case, energy is invested in searching for the "cause" of suffering in a misguided belief that finding this "cause" will take the suffering away. Again this is a futile trap that leads nowhere and can destroy relationships in the process. Many times this strategy only adds to the burden of suffering that has occurred, turning a difficult situation into a nearly impossible one.

Recall the behavior of the narcissistic leader as mentioned in the previous chapter for an extreme image of this response to suffering. The unbridled ego simply cannot take responsibility for anything that goes wrong and insists on blaming another, even if it destroys the other person or organization. The desire of the wounded ego to protect itself from suffering can be severe and can wreak havoc on everything in its path.

A slightly more positive response of the ego to suffering, though still ineffective, is to rush in to "fix" the problem and take the pain away, which was my reaction to the suffering I witnessed at the shelter clinic. While I had experienced some success with lessening suffering for my hospice patients, I was encountering a different type of distress in the shelter—and my "helping" methods didn't work. The problem occurred when I tried to take away the pain of my patients rather than just sitting with their discomfort and being a strong witness for them. My kindness was needed, as Ben reminded me, but not so much my "helping" behaviors that came from my desire to "do" rather than to "be."

Thus, the ego is rather limited in its view of suffering, because it focuses primarily on what has been damaged or lost and the ensuing pain that occurs. Ultimately however the ego can learn through repeated experiences with suffering and begin to grow in resilience and the capacity to tolerate difficulties. This can be a slow process that leaves behind many scars, but we are designed to learn and grow over time, so even without the awareness of the Soul, the ego can make great progress. However, there is one more sinister and hidden trap to keep in mind.

TRAVEL ADVISORY

Once again it is important to remember the tendency of the ego to hijack the spiritual growth process and use it for its own ends. While the ego initially protests and struggles when difficulties occur, sooner or later it turns to other strategies, particularly when it has been left to its own devices within the Shadow. Eventually, even after a setback that has knocked it down to the ground, the ego regains composure and begins to ask its central question, "What's in this for me?" Without supervision from the wiser, more-knowing Soul, the ego can take over the suffering process and use it to gain power and control over other people.

If the source of pain cannot be eliminated by blaming another or finding a cause, then the unchecked ego will eventually find ways to utilize the pain for self-serving purposes. This results in a state of perpetual victimhood or "living in the wound," as the ego parades its suffering around, demanding special treatment and privileges because it has such a sad story to tell.

While there's nothing wrong with receiving empathy or support from others when one is suffering, the problem with allowing the ego to be in charge of gathering that support is that the ego is inherently selfish. So empathy will be demanded from others, but none given in return. And the ego has little interest in growth or learning, so those processes will stop while the ego feeds itself on the current sad state of suffering that exists. In fact, there is no incentive for growth to occur because the secondary rewards from this difficult situation are so great for the ego—therefore learning or gaining a new perspective become nearly impossible since they would only threaten the ego's coping mechanism.

The only way the ego is likely to be shaken from this type of stronghold is if the Soul is suddenly activated by an unexpected experience, like meeting a new person, for example. When the Soul is called forth it will immediately begin shining its light and exposing the fraudulent behavior of the ego, which is a threat close to death for the ego. A fierce battle might follow, while the ego tries to discredit the Soul, but the ego, ultimately will fail.

THE SOUL AND SUFFERING

Here's what the Soul knows about suffering that is so frightening for the ego: suffering doesn't really exist—it is only the *perception of suffering* that causes us pain. The Soul, as we are defining it, has the advantage of viewing life here in the Garden from the perspective of the Galaxy; and everything looks very different from that elevation. The Soul is aware of the entire Universe, which has existed for some 12-14 billion years, as far as we know; the Soul has an understanding of the whole history of humankind, which has been around for a few million years; and the Soul has been a keen observer of each and every moment of this one, brief lifetime of yours (and other lifetimes as well if those have existed.) So the Soul recognizes all the patterns of growth and transformation that are common to our earthly lives.

The Soul can see beyond each event that appears to be tragic here in the Garden and can perceive the larger view, the greater design that is being masterfully woven from

all the threads of energy throughout the entire Universe.

From this grand perspective, every event of life has the potential to assist us on our learning path—there is no "good" outcome or "bad" result, no right or wrong, no positive or negative. Everything in the Universe is connected in a flowing, pulsing surge of energy, and that is true here on this planet as well. Everything emerges from and returns to the same Source; everything expands and contracts in this breathing, living energy field; everything is part of the Whole, nothing is left out or a mistake. As for us, we have arrived here asleep and unaware of these mysteries of the Universe, even though that knowledge is within us at all times. Thus the purpose of our time here is to conduct this journey to learn what we actually already know but cannot yet perceive.

The inward journey primarily consists of gradually shedding every aspect of this existence that is not Real and True. Therefore we must be willing to let go of the majority of what we perceive to be reality if we are to progress on our journey. This dismantling and stripping away of false perceptions is deeply painful for the ego, which knows nothing else except those parts to which it clings. Often the ego must endure a great deal of loss all on its own, before it awakens to the Soul and can find soothing peace, at last, in that awareness. The Soul knows that this perceived suffering of our lives actually represents growth and progress toward what is Real and True. The Soul knows that resisting the pain only brings more pain; and that facing and embracing our difficulties with *fearless love* is the only way to reveal the ultimate Truth.

So in this Garden, where we have been asked to toil, we must endure and surmount great challenges, experience much pain, and ultimately lose everything that we had mistakenly thought mattered to us. But it is all perfect in its own way. And whenever we get a glimpse of this existence from the Galaxy view of the Soul, we can share, for just one moment, in the tinkling laughter of the Universe as our perceptions fall away and all suffering disappears. "Ah yes!" we will shout as we recognize what we have always known—for that one moment—until the clouds reappear and our sight is veiled once more. Then we will return to our inward journey through the Garden, pick up our tools and our packs as we prepare to move along a few more steps on the path, nurturing our bandaged places and gazing at them ... always, always ... waiting for the light.

TRANSFORMING YOUR LIFE

Start wherever you are on this journey of yours and recognize that suffering of some sort or another is a prerequisite for genuine spiritual growth. The ego must be gradually dismantled in order for your Soul to begin guiding your life. If things have already fallen apart for you then you are well on your way. Your suffering may seem unwarranted and unfair but it is what life has given to you—so the only choice that will lead you to transformation is to embrace your wounds and rise above them.

Ultimately you will help the entire planet when you become aware of the suffering of others and connect to their pain through your own. In order for humanity to transcend to a new consciousness the same process of falling apart, embracing the difficulties, and expanding to a new perspective is necessary. Don't underestimate the fact that your spiritual growth serves the growth of humankind. Commit to a daily practice as you proceed on your inward journey while you also navigate the challenges that currently threaten our world. In the midst of this darkness hope may seem to be just a thin ray of light. But keep going and trust that a breakthrough is coming and the light will never fail you.

TOOLS FOR THE JOURNEY

These tools will help you weather the disruptions and the ups and downs of your inward journey after things have fallen apart. They are intended to empower your Soul to bring forth its wisdom and guidance and to help the ego cope with its distress along the way. Kenji Miyazawa, a Japanese poet and author of children's literature wrote: "We must embrace pain and burn it as fuel for our journey." Remember that image as you work with your own suffering; see your own pain as dry sticks and leaves, kindling for the fire that will propel you along the way. Check the **Resources** page for these and other tools at www. eoluniversity.com/resources.

Mindset Shift

The Mindset Shift that is necessary to manage suffering involves learning to witness your challenges without being crushed by them. Learn to take one step back from your pain and view it from a distance as if you were a scientist observing a lab experiment. In your journal write about these questions:

- What is causing me pain or troubling me today?
- What is life asking me to embrace today?

When you spend some time writing about your current suffering from this positive perspective you will be acknowledging your own pain and not repressing it, but also shifting your viewpoint to look for the hidden gem within that difficulty. Describe the physical, emotional, mental and spiritual aspects of any suffering you are experiencing right now.

SHADOW WORK

Next, dig deep and search for any Shadow issues that might be associated with your discomfort. Consult your **Life Journey Map** to look for any events of the past that might be connected. Then journal about the 3 steps of Shadow work:

1. Recognize: Is this pain arising from something in the past that I haven't wanted to look at? How have I used the pain as an excuse to avoid taking responsibility for my life?

2. Recover: Where have I rejected and ignored myself? How can I love myself better?

3. Rise above: What can I learn from this painful experience?

Example: *If I am experiencing chronic back pain I will write down a physical description of the pain (stabbing and severe), how I am feeling about being in that constant pain (frustrated and irritable) and what I'm thinking about the pain (I shouldn't have lifted that heavy box). From my exploration of Shadow issues I recognize that my back pain is usually associated with pushing myself too hard physically, which I do to make up for feeling that I'm not "good enough." Next I will focus on loving the part of me that feels inadequate and then look at what spiritual lesson I can learn from this pain that might help me grow. I have come to see that my back pain is a sign that I am not taking care of myself and that the pain gives me an excuse to avoid situations where I fear I might not be good enough. When the pain* *returns in the future I can use it to remind me to slow down, to be more present in this moment, and to love myself even in times when I feel like a failure.*

PRACTICE

Use the **Self-Compassion Practice**, which you will find fully described on the **Resource Page**, to reinforce the wisdom of this lesson. In this exercise you visualize a ray of pure, white light entering through the top of your head and filling your heart with each inhale. Then you imagine the light radiating from your heart to the area where you are experiencing pain. You continue to visualize the warm light of love surrounding your pain until you feel the intensity of the pain begin to lessen. You can use this exercise any time you feel discomfort as it will help you embrace rather than reject or repress your pain.

Letting Go is another helpful imagery practice to use while you work on this lesson. Sit in a comfortable position with your eyes closed. Take some deep breaths then focus on your toes. First tense them for a few seconds then let them relax as you let go of the tension. Move on to your feet, calves, thighs, hands, arms, shoulders, etc. and progressively tense each muscle group then let go until you reach the top of your head. When your musculoskeletal body feels totally relaxed shift your focus within. Imagine a ball of fire burning inside you that is causing your pain. As you continue to take deep breaths see a gentle rain shower hovering over the fire and gradually dousing the flames until only ashes remain. Then with each exhalation imagine blowing away the ashes to let go of your pain until you feel peaceful emptiness inside.

. . .

ACTION STEP

Finally the Action Step that can help you more deeply ingrain this lesson of suffering is to **Talk to Your Pain**. Each day as you wake up and become aware of the pain say something like "Hello grief (or back pain or broken heart.) I see you are still with me today. I will carry you until you have finished your work." This statement acknowledges that you are not denying your pain and that you recognize something valuable can come from pain. You don't have to say it aloud because thinking these words is equally effective. The point of this exercise is to start the day by embracing your discomfort and allowing it to be part of your life for whatever benefit it may offer.

4. THE SECOND LESSON: LOVE

"Something opens our wings.
Something makes boredom and hurt disappear.
Someone fills the cup in front of us:
We taste only sacredness."

- RUMI

In this quote from Rumi we are introduced to the transformative power of Love: the "something" and "someone" that offers us the taste of sacredness. This is not the love that is portrayed in romantic movies or torrid novels. This is not a love that we can recognize in most aspects of our ordinary lives. This Love, which comprises the second lesson of our inward journey of spiritual transformation, is something far deeper and more profound than we can even conceptualize. This Love is the very force of creation that can change everything in an instant. When life has fallen apart and all our options have disappeared this Love reveals itself as the inspiration that lifts us above the damage to see the potential for growth and healing. This is the Love that breathes life into the Universe and makes every moment sacred.

THE LOVE PROJECT

As time went on in the little shelter clinic where I volunteered every Wednesday afternoon, I began to recognize that I needed to change my attitude and approach to the patients I was seeing. Ben's visit had inspired me to see the power of simple compassion and had also reminded me of a significant memory from the past:

When I was 16 years old my friend and classmate Jolene died suddenly in a fall that occurred while she was hiking in the mountains near our town. For the first time in my life I was confronted with the reality that someone my own age could die. While I had been plan-ning since the age of 12 that I would one day become a doctor I had never considered the possibility that I could actually die young and never complete that goal. I felt confused and somehow betrayed by the fickleness of life. What good was knowing my purpose if one false step could sweep it all away from me? I entered into a state of depression and doubt that caused me to consider giving up on my dream of being a doctor. But one day I awoke with an epiphany that Love is the only thing that really matters in this life; that learning how to give and receive Love was the real purpose for my existence. Medicine was just one of many paths I could take while I sought to fulfill my true purpose of Love. So I was inspired to continue working toward my earlier goal of medical school while I also started my own quest to learn about Love. I understood then that Love could become my most important tool as a doctor if indeed I was able to complete that journey and one day practice medicine. For I was learning that unconditional love is the most powerful healing force in existence.

Even though medical training and my father's suicide had called my beliefs into question over the years, I still knew, deep inside of myself, that Love—learning to give and receive it—was the purpose of my life, the very reason I came to the planet. These many years later, I was also being reminded by my work with hospice patients of the importance of love. Some of my patients had told me they finally recognized, while on their deathbeds, that love was the only thing that mattered to them. They wanted nothing more than to spend each of their final moments of life giving and receiving love with the people closest to them. And they wanted to remind everyone, including me, to just keep sharing love no matter what else happens in life.

Inspired by this memory from the past and the messages from my hospice patients I decided that this little shelter clinic was the perfect place to put to the test the theory that Love is a healing force. Just like that, the **Love Project** was born. For this project I decided to focus on sending pure, radiant love to each and every person I saw in the clinic rather than on trying to "fix" their lives. Of course I would still provide the same medical care I had been giving before but my intention would change and I would let go of thinking that I should have all the answers for each person. I wouldn't tell the patients I was sending them love, but I would visualize opening my heart and radiating as much unconditional love as possible. In this way I hoped I would become a mirror within which each woman could see the reflection of her own beautiful soul.

To accomplish this Love Project I would need to spend time in meditation each day filling my own heart with love so that it would overflow when I was in the clinic. Through my hospice work I had discovered "The Lovingkindness Blessing," which I was already using on a regular basis during meditation to open my heart. The Love Project was an exciting new approach to these challenging patients at the shelter clinic and would allow me to put my new spiritual practice into action each week. I started looking forward to going to the clinic every Wednesday to work on my project.

From the beginning however the Love Project seemed to be transforming me more than anyone else. I couldn't see much change in the patients after I sent them love, but I was developing a more positive attitude toward the clinic and I no longer felt at a loss or speechless when I encountered great suffering. I always knew exactly what to do—simply keep my heart open and send out the love I had been learning to give. With this new practice I became calmer and even more tolerant and compassionate in my behavior. And this change in me did not go totally unnoticed ... at least, not by Charlotte the retired nurse who volunteered at the little clinic with me every Wednesday afternoon.

Charlotte was from the "old-school" generation of nurses who were accustomed to being ordered around by egotistical, authoritarian doctors even though they, the nurses, were actually the ones running everything behind the scenes. My work style as a doctor had always been to treat nurses as equally valuable members of the care team rather than as my inferiors, but this made Charlotte uncomfortable and confused. She was in her seventies and had recently given up her job as the nursing director for our local hospital where she had a reputation for being a stern and uncompromising leader. Her no-nonsense approach to medicine was focused solely on good physical care of the patient and she had no experience with looking at the emotional or spiritual aspects of illness.

Right away after I started the Love Project she noticed that something had changed about the way I was interacting with patients —and she didn't like it at all.

"You're too nice to them," she would say, throwing up her hands in frustration after learning that yet another woman had left the shelter to go back home to the same abusive situation as before.

"They need to shape up and get their lives in order," she complained.

Charlotte could barely hold back her criticism and sometimes had to leave the room abruptly before she blurted out something judgmental and hurtful to a patient.

Of course, I didn't feel that I could tell Charlotte about the Love Project just as I hadn't been able to tell anyone during my medical training that I believed in the healing power of love. I knew that Charlotte would never understand my beliefs and I was already coping with a heavy load of disapproval from her. I often wondered what drew her to volunteer at the clinic in the first place, since she didn't seem to like the patients at all. Some days I would fantasize about how nice it would be to have a nurse working with me who was in on the Love Project and could join me in sending pure love to our patients. But, for whatever reason, Charlotte was the nurse who had stepped up to help me, every Wednesday afternoon, in the little two-room shelter clinic.

From week-to-week I couldn't really tell if the Love Project was having any impact. I just knew that I was much happier with my new focus. I could relax with each patient, knowing that I didn't have to fix her life or solve her problems, I could just sit with her and send pure love while I listened.

One day at the end of a clinic session Charlotte seemed particularly exasperated and said, "What's wrong with all these women? Why can't they just change?"

I came close to telling her about the Love Project at that moment, because I wanted her to find the same joy in working with these patients that I was discovering, but the timing wasn't right.

"They're just too broken inside right now, Charlotte," I responded and I saw a flicker of understanding in her eyes.

Her face softened and she sighed deeply, "I guess so."

But change is often hidden, happening under the surface where we cannot see. The chrysalis looks exactly the same on the outside every day of its existence, while amazing transformation is occurring silently within as the larva develops into a butterfly. And then, without *explanation, the chrysalis breaks away as something—some invisible force—finally opens the butterfly's wings.*

One day well into the Love Project, a young woman stopped by the clinic to say goodbye. Amanda was in her early twenties and had a two-year old son who had been housed at the shelter with her for the previous three months. During that time she had been able to find a job, secure a place to live, and do the psychological work necessary to split from her abusive boyfriend. So Amanda was leaving the shelter to start a brand new life. Because she and her son had been seen at the clinic several times over the course of her stay, she wanted to say goodbye to us before her departure.

Amanda sat on the exam table wearing denim overalls and with her hair twisted into two long braids, making her look even younger than her age. She told us about her plans and how excited she was to be launching a new start for herself and her son.

With a radiant smile she said, "The best part of all is that now I know what love is."

Her use of the word "love" grabbed my attention and I leaned toward her as she went on to explain, "All of my life, every person who ever said they loved me, also hit me. So I thought that being abused was part of love and I thought that was how I was supposed to treat my son, too. But coming here, I have felt truly loved for the first time in my life. Now I know what it means and how it feels to be loved. And now I can raise my son the right way."

She added, "Thank you for helping me change my life," as she gave Charlotte and me each a huge hug before walking out the door.

I was stunned—the Love Project had actually been working all along without my recognition. Charlotte stood there with a look of total surprise on her face and then, for the first time since we started volunteering together at the clinic, a very slight smile graced her lips. Her dream, and mine, had come true: one of our patients had changed her life, at last.

After that revelation from Amanda I proceeded with the Love

Project with even more confidence. Now I knew that for at least some patients, the seeds of transformation were being sown beneath the surface even when I couldn't see any growth from the outside. And it seemed to me that Charlotte might be softening just a tiny bit, as well, though she was still her crusty, abrasive self most of the time. But she complained a little less than before and stopped being critical of my kindness toward patients, which was a big relief to me.

A few months later another small breakthrough occurred for Charlotte. She had volunteered to stay in the exam room with me to hold a one-year old boy on her lap while I performed an examination on his mother. I glanced over and saw the little boy reach out his pudgy index finger to touch the tip of Charlotte's nose and then giggle mischievously. Totally charmed by this adorable child, Charlotte chuckled and smiled back at him as she touched his nose in return. This time the smile stayed on Charlotte's face for the rest of the day. Her heart had been opened just a crack by the spontaneous affection of that precious little boy. It was as if her cup had been filled and at last she was able to taste the sacredness—of love. Yes, the Love Project was working its hidden magic and things would not be the same again in the little two-room shelter clinic on Wednesday afternoons.

In this story I began to experiment with hidden ways to offer love to others because I had run out of options for "fixing" the suffering of the shelter patients. With no other reasonable alternatives in sight I was able to be of service to them by harnessing my growing capacity for *fearless love*, which I was learning through my work with dying patients in hospice. But my ego was still attached to the idea of seeing the "results" of the Love Project and I had to learn on multiple occasions that love works in unseen ways and I might never know if it made a difference or not. I remained inspired to continue the project because it was clearly good for *me*, which I appreciated on an ego level, and also because deep inside, my higher self kept whispering to me that it was the right thing to do. There was still much for me to learn about love on my inward journey—particularly how to stand up for love when others, like Charlotte, don't value it. But I would first have to practice loving myself so that I could become a more powerful container for the divine love that was "filling my cup." This would prove to be the ultimate challenge for me as my journey continued.

THE PATH OF LOVE

Once we are able to manage the difficulties of life with some equanimity and have begun to master the lesson of Suffering, we quickly move on to the next obstacle in our inward journey of spiritual development, which is the lesson of Love. The path of Love to an outsider may appear, well ... lovely ... but it is actually a harrowing expedition. The moment you open yourself to Love you may experience the joyful ecstasy of connecting deeply with another, but that connection exposes you inevitably to the risk of immeasurable despair when Love suddenly vanishes due to death, betrayal, or abandonment.

Love always comes closely tied to Suffering because Love is one of the causes of our deepest pain.

In popular culture romantic love is often portrayed as happy and fun, with beautiful, sexy couples strolling arm-in-arm along a beach, gazing into one another's eyes, kissing in the moonlight.

Those fantasy scenes rarely show the real work of genuine Love, which requires us to dig deep within ourselves, become naked and vulnerable to another, and risk utter devastation in the process. True Love is not for the faint-of-heart.

Ironically we spend much of our lifetimes searching for love, seeking to be loved and to know, unquestionably, that we are lovable, but we don't actually even understand this "love" that we seek. In 7 *Lessons for Living from the Dying* we saw that the giving and receiving of Love became the key to finding meaning in life for those who were approaching death, but many of those patients didn't appreciate or truly experience Love until they were in their last days of life.

For the most part our early definitions of love come from our experience with parents or other adults in our lives who supposedly love us—and, like Amanda in the story, we may be totally confused about the nature of this "love" that we encounter. While we can be deeply attached to our parents and family in childhood, we do not become capable of putting the needs of another ahead of our own until we are in later adolescence. But then sexual attraction and romance add even more confusion to our ideas of love. And to make things still more challenging, the English language has only one word for this feeling of "love" and we must use it to describe our positive feelings toward everything from chocolate cake to a brand of automobile to our soul-mate to God or the Divine. No wonder love seems so complicated at times!

Most of us eventually learn our own lessons about love when we enter into a relationship with another and begin to experience what it means to be "in love." Initially love attracts us with its shiny, bright appearance and promises of bliss. We are lured in by the trappings of love and become enamored with the *idea* of being in love. We can remain in the blissful, euphoric state of infatuation for quite some time. But then slowly the truth is revealed to us that, as an old Spanish proverb says, "Where there is love, there is pain."

What we discover as we proceed more deeply along this road of love is that love is designed to be one of life's greatest difficulties even while it is also a source of pure joy.

Deep relationships often become challenging because they push us into unknown territory where confusion reigns and the Shadow can emerge. When we enter into a love relationship for the first time, we lack pre-patterned and conditioned modes of behavior and we find ourselves forging a new path with each step we take in this risky venture. We can become vulnerable to collapse while we are learning to love another deeply. And we do collapse many times, over and over again, and ask ourselves "Why? Why am I here? Why am I part of such a relationship?" This is the point at which we discover that love has a great deal to teach us if we are willing to allow our hearts to be broken and our lives to fall apart.

In my own history, when it became clear to me at age sixteen that I should devote my life to learning about love, I set about studying the theory of love and all things related to love. However I did not realize that I would never truly *know* love until I embodied it and practiced it in my life. That part of my education came much later, when I began to master the vast wisdom provided by the experience of deep and fearless love.

THE WISDOM OF LOVE

"You have to keep breaking your heart
until it opens."

-RUMI

The difficult truth about Love on the inward journey is that it is meant to break us so that we can open our hearts and grow to our highest potential. Our deepest relationships of love provide us with the best possible opportunities to encounter some of the wounds that reside in the Shadow. For we soon discover that true love often leads to conflict that is triggered by old unhealed pain. When that pain finally comes to the surface we have a chance to start healing it and to reclaim and re-own parts of ourselves that have been disconnected for much of our lives. If we are able to stay on the dangerous journey of true love without giving up and ending the situation or relationship, we can continue to grow and heal. By this process of clearing out old wounds we create more openness and spaciousness within and become more and more our most authentic selves. But love is never an easy road to travel.

Ultimately, our work to learn how to love becomes a pathway of service, a means of showing devotion for all of life. Rumi wrote, "In every religion there is love, yet love has no religion." Love is meant to break down barriers and cross all boundaries when we are able to share it from a position of strength and confidence. For me this happened when I began utilizing love as a tool of service within the shelter clinic. All of the healing that I had encountered in my life through my own heart-breaking love relationships had shaped me into a vessel for love that could be transmitted to others. When our hearts are broken open they allow the light of love to shine through so that others can see it and be blessed by it. This was the ultimate outcome of the Love Project.

The suffering we encounter when we take the risk of loving others actually hollows us out inside and opens our own channels through which love can freely flow. When we allow this clearing out process to take place we accept the opportunity to learn the deep wisdom of love and we transform ourselves into vessels of love. The fewer internal obstacles we have, the more purely we can transmit love to others and share the healing process with them. This is precisely the gift the entire world needs from each of us: to be our own authentic channels of love that can heal and nurture the wounds of this planet. When we allow love to break us and shape us then we step fully into our purpose in this lifetime.

Mother Theresa said, "I have found the paradox, that if you love until it hurts, there can be no more hurt, only more love." When we give our love freely, we can enjoy the fruits of love, such as seeing another person grow and transform with that love. But as long as we still have Shadow wounds within us that need to heal, we will continue to experience the pain and suffering brought by love. Our own process of growth will keep cycling and spiraling upward as we move forward in love.

But for many of us the most difficult task is actually learning self-love because we have been taught that to care for ourselves ahead of others is selfish and wrong. The problem with this theory is that we cannot share love if we have not first mastered how to carry love. And to carry love we must be certain that we are worthy of love. Self-loathing creates a small and leaky vessel that cannot hold or transmit clear, pure love to another person. So on our inward journeys we must overcome our own internal judgements from the ego and receive the very Love from the Soul that we long to give to others. The goddess Durga can bring her *fearless love* to life because she has harnessed the power of the tiger to transport her and support her efforts. Like Durga we need to become fearless in our love for ourselves if we are going to change the world in a powerful way. When everything falls apart we must not run away or blame ourselves but recognize the opportunity before us to take a step toward love.

DETOURS ALONG THE ROAD

We must always remember however that there are many potential detours that can trap us and lead us off the path on this inward journey of Love. Often we will not recognize these pitfalls until we have strayed far away from love and become entangled with negative beliefs and emotions that distract us and drain our energy. As we have already seen, these detours can also be opportunities for us to learn new dimensions of love, as long as they don't totally remove us from the journey of love.

One of the most challenging detours we can face as we learn about love is that of **betrayal and abandonment**. Eventually we will deeply love someone who is not capable of fully loving us in return. This unbalanced situation can cause deep pain and suffering for the one who has freely given love and can result in a belief that love itself has tricked or cheated us. This can lead to disillusionment and rejection of the whole journey of love and cause an avoidance of the "dangers of love" in the future. I have worked with many individuals who have lived alone for most of their adult lives, refusing to share love with anyone, because they were betrayed by a love relationship in the distant past. But betrayal is one of the dark lessons of love, designed to break the ego down and open the heart to compassion. We are asked to endure betrayal when it arrives in our lives so that we can learn never to betray another and particularly, never to betray ourselves. The danger of this detour occurs if we choose to be cut off from love entirely rather than take the risk of being hurt.

Another common pitfall along this path of love is **loneliness**. Sometimes we are asked to learn about deep love by being without it in our lives for prolonged periods of time. We may become bitter and cynical about love when it doesn't seem to be gracing us with its presence, but often we can learn a great deal during these painful times. When love seems to be absent we can study it from a distance and truly appreciate the positive difference love brings to us. We can also examine our own capacity for love and work on our wounds and flaws that may be interfering with the free flow of love through us to the world. And often we are being asked to learn how to love ourselves first before we connect with another person who needs our love.

However, we also need to learn that love is actually all around us and within us and we need only be open to it in order to experience it in our day-to-day lives. Sometimes being deprived of a deep intimate relationship becomes an opportunity to give love to the world in a larger sense. So loneliness is a detour that cannot be avoided but can be utilized for positive growth when we refuse to be defeated by its occurrence as part of our journey. The solution for loneliness is to remember to "Find the Love" in everything around you.

Finally, when the Shadow is powerful we can get caught in a detour of **Shadow love**, such as Amanda in the story at the beginning of this chapter. She gave her love freely to an abusive man because she misunderstood the nature of love. We can also be trapped by our love for a destructive habit or an addictive substance or behavior. In each of these cases we are practicing a form of love but it is arising from unhealed wounds in the Shadow aspect of our ego. This type of love does not bring healing and transformation but keeps us trapped in a prison of misery. Such a detour can last for years until an opportunity for genuine love occurs.

As mentioned before, detours along the path of love are normal and to be expected as part of the inward journey. But we need to be aware of the places where we might be led astray so that we can take care and stay mindful on the path. In that way we will be able to utilize our detours as true learning opportunities that can deepen our experience of love overall.

THE EGO AND LOVE

At the lowest functioning level of the self (body/mind and ego), love is an asset or even a commodity to be sought after, gathered, hoarded, rationed, shared or denied by the "owner." At this level love can also be exchanged for happiness and wellbeing and withheld in order to punish someone else. From this perspective, love is either the most wonderful, advantageous experience of life or the most miserable, overrated state of existence, and the ego may career back and forth between these two extremes.

The ego is primarily focused on **getting and receiving love** as a survival mechanism. In fact love seems like a great idea to the ego as long as it is receiving all the positive benefits of love from someone else. The ego can also be willing to give love with the assurance of receiving it in return when the exchange seems fair and balanced. But the ego quickly becomes miserable whenever there is a disruption in love or an occurrence of one of the natural ups and downs in a relationship. Love can only be an acceptable option for the ego if it makes life better and is reciprocated to an equal degree.

In fact, love appears to be a solution to the emptiness the lower self feels inside and the ego will attempt to "fill up" that hole by getting and giving love. However, as we have already seen, that internal "hole" will never be filled until the ego is capable of recognizing the Soul, which is the only thing that can resolve the emptiness inside. So love is really part of the *path* that leads toward this recognition of the Soul—and superficial love itself cannot fill the emptiness; love is a *process* and not the ultimate destination. We will continue to seek love from outside of ourselves to make us feel whole until we are actually capable of recognizing that "You have within you more love than you could ever understand," as Rumi wrote—we already contain all of the love that we are seeking from others.

However, the ego is also capable of growing in the capacity to give and receive love. The path of spiritual growth consists of gradually breaking down the barriers to love so that the self becomes a more and more pure vessel for transmitting love out to the world. We are drawn to love over and over again by our own hearts, which are ultimately broken open by the act of loving. But this brokenness becomes exactly the vehicle we need in order to grow spiritually and to bring our gifts to the world.

Documentary filmmaker Michelle LeBrun, whose film *Death: A Love Story* chronicles the process of illness and eventual death of her husband Mel, describes in the film how she was gradually broken open as she sat with Mel during his final days of life and watched him fade away. Michelle later said, "It's that tenderheartedness, brokenheartedness that I really try and carry through my life ... Brokenheartedness and compassion allow you to hold the space for others to be the best possible that they can be." Michelle teaches us that allowing our hearts to be broken by love changes us forever, but it is one of the keys to becoming our own best selves and to supporting the growth of others, as well.

TRAVEL ADVISORY

> *"The beginning of love is to let those we love be perfectly themselves, and not twist them to fit our own image. Otherwise we love only the reflection of ourselves we find in them."*
>
> -THOMAS MERTON

As we have seen before, the ego has its own deceptive means of taking over the process of spiritual growth and love is one of the aspects of our growth that can be hijacked without our awareness. The ego initially resists the idea of genuine love for another because love requires vulnerability through allowing our protective barriers to come down. But if the ego recognizes that love can serve its goals and desires, then it may engage in a "take-over" of the process of love and create a relationship driven by lower egoic desires.

Those who love us can serve as mirrors, reflecting back to us an image of our own likeness. Much like the character Narcissus from Greek mythology, the ego can actually fall in love with its own reflection that it sees in the eyes and face of another, rather than genuinely loving the other person for him or herself. Then the ego may appear to be engaging in love, but in reality, the love being generated is for its own superficial appearance—there is no genuine recognition of the other person or appreciation for the uniqueness of that person. In this way, the ego can fool the lower self into believing that it is practicing love, but it is a masquerade that actually demeans and devalues, rather than nurtures and supports, the other person. This narcissistic love does not foster growth or deepen spiritual awareness and ultimately does not last. It is a common foible of those still immature in the practice of love and needs to be recognized and overcome as we progress on our spiritual journeys.

THE SOUL AND LOVE

> *"If the house of the world is dark, Love*
> *will find a way to create windows."*

-RUMI

Ultimately from the highest perspective possible, which is the view taken by the Soul or True Self, Love is none other than Divine energy, the creative force that can transform the entire world. For the Soul, love is less personal and more Universal—so the Soul does not engage in the drama of superficial romance. Love is consistent and somewhat detached for the Soul as it continually flows from the Divine Source, through our human forms, out to the world.

When the walls and the obstacles of the lower self have been broken down, then this Divine energy can flow freely through us as earthly "transport vessels" for love. That Divine love is shaped by the unique characteristics of each individual through which it flows—therefore the love that *you* bring to the world will differ from the love that *I* present to others, even though the Source of love is the same for both of us. Our individual "models" of love are formed by our strengths, as well as our flaws and scars, so that the love we each carry is exactly what is needed by the world.

For the Soul, the more we become our authentic selves in this lifetime, the more we will allow the free flow through us of Divine *fearless love* that can heal the world.

So the Soul does not rush in to protect the lower self from being broken by love—the Soul stands back and allows the destruction to happen, knowing that it is a necessary step. The Soul awaits greater and greater opening within us, more hollowness, more expansiveness, more emptiness, so that love can fill all the spaces as it pours through us and out to the world. This is the *harsh grace* borne by the Soul: the knowledge that the journey to spiritual growth requires this devastating and destructive journey through love, where love is both the answer to our pain and the cause of our pain at the same time.

Yet, in the midst of our deepest darkness, we can trust that our wings will be opened, our cup will be filled, and we will one day know only the sacredness of love.

TRANSFORMING YOUR LIFE

You are here to be a vessel for fearless love and the suffering you have endured has opened you to carry even more compassion and light for the world. Recognize that your greatest challenge will be to learn to love the "unlovable" people in your life. This includes being able to love the planet and people far away whose actions you do not understand. Part of this journey of love includes simple acts of compassion such as wearing a mask and maintaining a safe distance during a pandemic; or reducing your personal "carbon footprint" when the planet is suffering a climate crisis.

Begin by searching your own Shadow for all that you do not love about yourself—for whatever you reject within yourself you will reject in others. This Shadow work has to be ongoing as you peel away your hidden self-loathing like the layers of an onion. When you begin to feel a glimmer of self-love you will naturally extend that love to others and find it easier to care about those who are different from you.

Look for the good, the "Divine light," in every person. Remember that there are no "throw-away" people—everyone matters and everyone deserves to be loved. If you share genuine love with the people you encounter in your day-to-day existence you will set in motion a ripple effect that will change the world.

TOOLS FOR THE JOURNEY

This lesson on the inward journey focuses on how you utilize *fearless love* in your day-to-day life. Opportunities for you to practice this love might occur in a relationship, but also exist in your work, your daily spiritual practice, or the simple tasks of daily living. Recognize that love is a powerful creative force that is present at all times whether or not you have a specific "love partner." Your ability to carry and channel this *fearless love* to others is influenced first of all by your openness to receiving love, which requires that you cultivate a sense of self-acceptance and worthiness. Next you will learn to let that love flow through you to others. Check the **Resources** page for these and other tools at www.eoluniversity.com/resources.

MINDSET SHIFT

The Mindset Shift that is necessary in order to practice *fear-*

less love is to understand that love is not something you seek outside of yourself but something that is always already within you. Rumi wrote: "Your task is not to seek love, but merely to seek and find all the barriers within yourself that you have built against it." Use your journal to explore these questions:

- What are the barriers within me to love?
- What needs to be opened and healed so that I can give and receive love more fully?

Shadow Work

Review your **Life Journey Map** and consider where love or the absence of love has been a factor on your journey. Make note of the times when love may have shifted your course and whether it led to joy or pain. Next consider the conflicts you have experienced in your relationships and explore the 3 steps of Shadow work in your journal:

1. Recognize: What factors have triggered my emotions and disrupted my relationships recently? When have I experienced similar disruptions in the past and what wounds or trauma are connected to those emotions?

2. Recover: What parts of myself do I find it difficult to love? How can I bring more love to these wounded parts?

3. Rise above: How might I change course in the future when my emotions are triggered? What healthier responses can I practice when conflicts occur in my relationships?

Example: I *have **recognized** my own tendency to lash out at other people when they offer me constructive criticism and I'm* *aware that it comes from a lack of self-esteem that began in child-hood. To **recover** I will practice loving the wounded child within me and becoming more aware of my own inner critic. Then to **rise above** my old Shadow behavior I will reframe criticism as positive and motivating instead of painful and destructive.*

PRACTICE

One useful Practice to expand your capacity for love is this **Fearless Love Meditation**, which you can find in full on the **Resource Page** and can utilize as an addition to the **Letting Go** practice from the previous lesson. Begin the meditation practice with several deep breaths. As your body begins to relax envision breathing in love with each inhale. See the love, like rays of light, entering you and filling in all the emptiness within you, occupying all the space you have cleared by the letting go practice. Recognize that you now have an even greater capacity to hold and carry love because you have released what doesn't serve you. Continue "filling" yourself with love until you sense that you are overflowing with love's light and energy. If you have identified a specific area within your physical or emotional body that needs some healing, such as I did with my back pain and my issue with criticism, focus on breathing love and its healing light into that area.

Next allow the love to flow from you like rays of light, radiating out as spirals that form larger and larger circles as they expand. Envision those spirals of light traveling to the people dearest to you and see them bathed in light. See the spirals of light continue to grow and extend farther and farther—to your neighbors, your entire community, your nation, your continent, the entire planet. There is no end to this fluid light of love. You can spread and share it endlessly and it will never expire or be exhausted. Focus the love on specific people or situations that you know can benefit from extra love right now.

ACTION STEP

Finally an Action Step to reinforce the lesson of *fearless love* is to get acquainted with your **Best Self,** an exercise adapted from the work of medical hypnotherapist Roger Moore.[1] Make a list of your best qualities and imagine how you would behave if you were always acting as the best person you could possibly be. Envision this greater version of you and study everything about yourself: how do you dress, speak, treat other people, spend your day? Write down three sentences that describe your highest self to post on your wall or bulletin board where you can see it every day. Or you might also draw a picture of this self you have envisioned. Remember this best version of you throughout the day and in difficult situations ask yourself: How would the better me handle this?

5. THE THIRD LESSON: FORGIVENESS

*"When you begin to see
that your enemy is suffering,
that is the beginning of insight."*

-THICH NHAT HAHN

I n this quotation, Vietnamese Zen master, Thich Nhat Hahn, describes the importance of connecting with the suffering of others, including our enemies, on this path toward spiritual growth. Of course, he is introducing the challenging concept of Forgiveness, which is the third lesson that ultimately must be mastered along this inward journey. When everything falls apart in life there can be many circumstances and individuals to blame for what has happened. The challenge is to rise above blame and see the bigger picture, which brings us closer to genuine insight and enlightenment. When we choose not to blame others for the events of our lives we find it increasingly difficult to identify them as enemies. Consider the question, "Who is your enemy?" as you contemplate the many faces of Forgiveness in this story.

FEEDING THE ENEMY

I arrived at the shelter clinic a little late one Wednesday afternoon to find Charlotte already exasperated with our first patient. She shoved the chart in my hand with a huff as she spat out, "See if you can talk any sense into her."

At 54-years of age, Kathryn was one of the shelter's older clients, who was brought in by the police after an argument with her husband had turned violent. He had shoved her and hit her several times and the neighbors, hearing shouts and screams coming through their bedroom window, had called 911. According to Kathryn this sort of violent outburst had never occurred before in the 30 years of her marriage and she was deeply embarrassed to be in this situation. She sat on the exam table wearing a neatly ironed skirt and jacket and clutching her purse close to her chest.

As she continued with her story, Kathryn revealed to me the information that had so upset Charlotte: she was planning to go back home to her husband when she left the shelter in a few days.

When I asked her why she would even consider such a thing, Kathryn said simply, "Because I love him … and I forgive him."

Forgiveness was not a concept that was discussed at the shelter. Most of the women who came there were so disempowered and beaten down that the counselors had to focus on rebuilding their self-esteem and shoring up their self-confidence just to help them function in the world again. These women needed to uncover their anger and find their power in order to move on with their lives. To the counselors at the shelter, forgiveness was not an act of healing and strength, but represented a dangerous sign of submissiveness and low self-esteem. So hearing Kathryn say that she forgave her husband that day in the clinic was a bit of a surprise for me and I understood why the counselors and Charlotte were so upset with her choice.

But in my other work with hospice patients, forgiveness was a common theme. Most of the patients I cared for were working diligently to let go of old resentments from the past before they died. I knew that forgiveness was an issue of great importance, but it wasn't addressed at the shelter because it wasn't appropriate for most of the clients. So I felt conflicted about how to respond to Kathryn's announcement that she had forgiven her abusive husband. Was forgiveness always necessary? Should some transgressions never be forgiven? Thinking about Kathryn's situation stirred up some of my own memories of learning the lessons of forgiveness:

*When I was very young my mother used to read the Bible to me every night before I went to sleep. I honestly didn't understand much of what she read, but one very interesting verse stuck in my head all throughout my childhood: "'Vengeance is mine, I will repay,' says the Lord. 'But if your enemy is hungry, feed him, and if he is thirsty, give him a drink; for in so doing **you will heap burning coals on his head**.'" (Romans 12:19)*

When I asked Mom what that meant she said that if we are nice to people who hurt us, then God will punish them—or at least that's what I understood her to say. I found this idea rather appealing— having God's wrath at my disposal to punish the people I didn't like— because I had a streak of vindictiveness within me, even at a young age. The next day I went to school and found my archenemy, a girl named Maria who used to harass me on the playground during recess. When I announced to her that I was going to be nice to her so that God would heap burning coals on her head she seemed a little frightened and started avoiding me. This "burning coals" idea appeared to be working out well and I often thought of it whenever I was angry at someone.

"Just wait until the burning coals come," I would think to myself as I imagined getting ultimate revenge on anyone who hurt or disappointed me.

Then many years later, during a college class that focused on the Old and New Testaments, I learned something new about the "burning coals" concept when we studied the actual verse that I had cherished since childhood. The professor, who delighted in debunking misconceptions about Biblical teachings, explained that the phrase "heap burning coals on their heads" actually referred to an old custom of giving visitors a bag of hot coals to sleep with at night to help them stay warm. Rather than representing torture or punishment, the burning coals were instead a gift of hospitality extended in good will!

This news came as a great surprise and disappointment to me: all of my past gloating over achieving revenge against people who had mistreated me had been totally misguided. God wasn't harming them on my behalf—He was welcoming them in with open arms, giving them shelter from the cold. This revelation completely altered my view of the world and rearranged all my thinking about revenge and vindictiveness. I now had a new concept to grapple with—that of ultimate forgiveness for wrongdoing. From that day forward I could no longer assume that there was a God who would punish others just because I thought it was a good idea. Everything was totally different than I had understood and for the first time I realized that in addition to my study of love I would need to learn about forgiveness, as well.

Several years later I had another opportunity to consider these ideas of vengeance and forgiveness. During my residency training I had a very difficult relationship with Christine, the head nurse of the Emergency Room where I was doing a rotation. For reasons I didn't understand at the time she disliked me intensely and took every possible opportunity to criticize my work, including my punctuality, my attitude, and my care of patients. I didn't recognize the depth of her negative feelings toward me until the end of my rotation in her *department when she wrote a letter to my residency director and recommended that I be dismissed from the program because of my "poor performance."*

I was called before the administration of the residency program and had to defend myself against multiple accusations—all of which I felt were based on misunderstandings and miscommunication. Fortunately I had a good relationship with the residency director who told me that Christine had complained about other residents in the past that she had disliked for one reason or another. He decided to ignore the letter and asked me to try to make amends with her. But I was upset and humiliated and chose instead to avoid her at all costs. I was finished with my rotation in the ER so I stayed away from that department and made sure I would never encounter Christine again. Meanwhile I silently seethed inside at the thought that she had tried to ruin my medical career for no good reason.

Several months later when I was on call in the hospital I heard that Christine, my sworn enemy, had been brought in for emergency surgery due to a ruptured ovarian cyst. She had apparently lost a lot of blood before she got to the hospital and could have died without quick intervention. Many thoughts and emotions swirled through my head when I heard that news: my old vindictive self was pleased that "karma" had played out and she was finally being punished for harming me.

However, at the same time I was also aware of a feeling of deep compassion for her. It didn't make sense to me, but I had a strange urge to take her a bouquet of flowers. I tried to ignore that idea, but it kept coming back to me, getting stronger and stronger each time I thought of it. I knew that Christine was single and had no family in the area. It was also clear that she was rather unpopular at work and had few friends. Suddenly I felt great concern for her—recovering from potentially life-threatening surgery all alone, with not one person to care about her welfare. Although I was still angry with her, I could also see her suffering and feel the pain that she was experiencing. Again I sensed a strong urge to buy flowers for her and then the Bible verse came to mind: "if your enemy is hungry, feed him, and if he is thirsty, give him a drink."

It was obvious to me that I needed to forgive Christine for writing that letter, but buying flowers for her seemed like too much to expect of me. I resisted the idea all day long, until finally at 8:59 pm, just before the hospital gift shop closed, I gave up the fight and stopped in to buy a beautiful bouquet of mixed flowers. Swallowing my pride and my fear, I walked into Christine's hospital room where I found her resting and alone—with no visitors, no cards, and no other flowers. As I stood next to the bed, she stared at me with a shocked look on her face, unable to say a word.

I was equally in shock but I managed to choke out: "I brought these flowers to tell you that I hope you recover quickly. I'm sorry this happened to you."

I placed the flowers on her nightstand and left the room as fast as I could, before she could say anything to me. Trembling with emotion as I walked down the hall I felt a weight being lifted off my shoulders and a smile of relief coming to my face. I was letting go of the bitterness and resentment I had been storing up for months and it felt wonderful to me. My hatred of Christine had been poisoning me for all that time and now I was being detoxified. Everything would be better now for me and also for Christine. "Burning coals" were being heaped on her head and perhaps she would know that she belonged and was being welcomed by the loving arms of the Divine.

Oddly, I never saw her again after that night. In a few months I graduated from residency and went into my own private practice where I quickly forgot about all of the struggles and traumas of those days of training. But her name was mentioned a year or so later, when I was taking a history from a new patient and asked how she had found me.

"Oh, Christine the head nurse in the Emergency Room recom-

mended you to me. She told me you were the best doctor in the entire county."

Hearing that comment, I felt a rush of joy as the final remnant of anger and resentment was lifted from me. For the first time I understood the power of forgiveness to transform a situation, a life, a relationship. Even though no words of forgiveness had been spoken between us and I hadn't seen Christine again after that night, the simple act of bringing her flowers—even with my reluctance—had been enough to precipitate healing for both of us.

As I listened to Kathryn describe her willingness to forgive her husband on that day in the little shelter clinic, I understood exactly what she was talking about. She explained that she knew every detail of her husband's life story, she was familiar with his pain and the wounds he carried from childhood—and she was the only person in his life who could help him heal. She recognized that her ability to forgive him, which arose from her deep love for him, was exactly what was necessary for him to change his life. She could offer him the "burning coals" he needed to feel warm and loved. She could use compassion and forgiveness to transform him from a reviled enemy into a welcome guest.

And as I looked at Kathryn through eyes of love, I could see that she was indeed strong in her ability to give genuine love and that her motivation to forgive was an impetus that came from her love, not a desperate sign of low self-esteem. In that moment, I knew that I should validate her feelings and offer my support for her decision to return home even though I couldn't predict the outcome of her choice. Of course I couldn't know if Kathryn had made the best decision for her life because she alone felt the inner guidance that led her to that, but I could sense that she was acting from the strength of her love.

As Kathryn walked out of the clinic that day, Charlotte scowled at me with disapproval—a reaction I knew the shelter counselors would share.

"You didn't talk her out of going home?" Charlotte sputtered in disbelief.

"She genuinely loves him ... and forgives him," I responded, unable to explain my thinking to her in a way she would understand.

As Charlotte stormed out of the room, she replied with heavy sarcasm and disdain, *"'Love? Forgiveness?' Oh please ... that's the most ridiculous thing I've ever heard."*

I sighed with fatigue, knowing that I had a long way to go before I could tell Charlotte or anyone else about the Love Project and the effect I thought it was having in the little two-room shelter clinic on Wednesday afternoons. And there was still a great deal for me to learn on this journey as well. I had not yet recognized my own need to forgive my father for taking his life or to forgive myself for all of my past failures. But that opportunity would come in its own time ...

In this story I was struggling to learn about the most challenging aspects of forgiveness, particularly the question of who should be forgiven and when and how to practice forgiveness. If the ultimate act of love is to love the unlovable, then the highest form of forgiveness must be to forgive the unforgivable. Indeed many of my hospice patients were working on forgiveness to this depth—finally letting go of anger over unforgivable wrongs that had taken place in the past. But I was learning that forgiveness requires a difficult journey with many stops along the way, and it cannot be undertaken until the basic tenets of the previous lesson of Love have been mastered.

Kathryn's story raised many issues about the nature of forgiveness and the balance between love for others and love for oneself. The only reason forgiveness was an acceptable path for Kathryn in the story is because she had already learned how to give and receive love and she had gained enough strength and power within herself to have compassion for her husband's suffering. Most of the other women at that shelter were still struggling to attain enough self-esteem and self-love to survive in this harsh world. For them, forgiveness was a lesson that would not be appropriate until much further down the road in their journeys. Forgiveness is a process that unfolds over time and cannot be rushed, which is why my own ultimate act of forgiveness for my father hadn't taken place yet.

THE PATH OF FORGIVENESS

"We pardon to the extent that we love."

-FRANCIS DE LA ROCHEFOUCAULD

In *7 Lessons for Living from the Dying* we also saw that the lesson of Forgiveness is closely tied to the lesson of Love, for everyone and everything that we love will ultimately disappoint us or cause us pain. We cannot strengthen our ability to love until we learn how to forgive, therefore these two lessons often confront us simultaneously. Through the act of forgiveness we learn to deepen our commitment to another and to make ourselves even more vulnerable. Forgiveness can help heal our broken and wounded hearts but also exposes them to the risk of additional pain as we continue on the path. Of course, we are never asked to put ourselves in an unsafe situation or to jeopardize our wellbeing for the sake of love or forgiveness. That is why forgiveness was not an appropriate topic for most of the women at the shelter. They would only be ready to forgive those who had harmed them when they were strong enough to protect themselves and stay away from toxic relationships.

Sometimes forgiveness is best offered from a distance such as when we look back at our lives from further along the road on our inward journeys. In my case I later began to understand why Christine had hated me so much during my residency. She was a devout Mormon and I was a single woman who practiced no religion even though I was exploring spirituality on my own. My values and lifestyle were far different from Christine's and she couldn't understand me or relate to me as a woman in medicine. Likewise I didn't understand Christine at all and had secretly judged her to be someone not worth knowing. I had done nothing to reach out to her until the night I dropped off the flowers. At that time I didn't recognize that I was responsible for my own behavior toward others who are different from me and also for how I showed myself to them. I realize now that many of our relationship conflicts arise from this inability to truly "see" the other person, the one we have identified as an enemy. Forgiveness requires us to dig deep into our Shadow wounds to clear them away and clean the "glass" through which we view others in order to see what is True. Taking flowers to Christine was just the first step in my journey toward forgiveness.

We first encounter the concept of forgiveness in childhood, as I did when my mother read Bible verses to me. But early on, our ability to truly forgive is limited because we are not yet capable of genuinely caring about the welfare of others. Then what we might call "forgiveness" can actually be a weapon we use to secretly punish the other person, like the "burning coals" I enjoyed heaping on my enemies. We must actively choose to deepen our understanding of forgiveness and work to develop the willingness to face and then release our resentments if we are going to master this lesson. Life offers us multiple opportunities to practice forgiveness through our relationships and experiences and in each situation the choice is ours, whether to hold onto or let go of anger.

If we grow in consciousness on this journey we may begin to practice more genuine forgiveness and offer it to others as a release from blame for something they've done wrong. However, most of us (about 60% of Americans according to a Fetzer Institute survey on forgiveness)[1] believe that forgiveness should only be offered after the offender has apologized and taken steps to make amends. And furthermore, 50% of people surveyed believe that there are situations that should *never* be forgiven. At this level of consciousness we are willing to practice forgiveness as a barter or an exchange for atonement, but only when our terms have been met.

Next our ongoing growth in conscious awareness brings us to a level where forgiveness takes on a new meaning and has a higher purpose: forgiveness becomes a blessing that is bestowed on another and, as we shall see, contains the potential for healing. Few of us are able to practice forgiveness from this higher perspective, because it requires letting go of blame toward others and releasing the desire for vengeance. In the story, I held my feelings of resentment toward Christine for several months before an opportunity arose for me to begin the work of forgiveness. And when I was finally shown that she was suffering, the impetus to forgive came to life inside of me. Even though I was initially reluctant to follow the inner guidance that led me toward that task, I was at a place in my own spiritual development where it was as hard to refuse a difficult lesson as it was to fulfill the lesson.

Just as we saw in *7 Lessons for Living from the Dying,* a physical action or gesture can be the catalyst for letting go of resentment—and so taking a bouquet of flowers to Christine was the act that allowed me to open and begin the release of my stored negative emotion toward her. That simple act and the passage of time ultimately transformed her opinion of me, in return.

While Forgiveness sounds very difficult to accomplish, the walls of hatred and loathing can collapse quickly when a genuine gesture of peace is offered. I never knew the outcome of Kathryn's relationship with her husband, but I know that she never returned to the shelter. It is possible that her willingness to forgive him, which arose from her deep love, could have been the very catalyst he needed to heal his wounds from the past. Forgiveness has the power to create miracles in our lives.

THE WISDOM OF FORGIVENESS

> *"To forgive is to set a prisoner free and discover that the prisoner was you."*
>
> -LEWIS B. SMEDES

Life will offer each of us many opportunities to learn the wisdom of Forgiveness, because it is one of the most important lessons we can master. Over and over again we will face disappointments, betrayals, losses, attacks, and insults that will push us to our limits and demand that we go deeper and broader with our understanding of forgiveness. But as we have seen, Forgiveness is linked to Love and mastering the practice of forgiveness will also assist us as we seek to bring Love into the world through the way we live our lives.

On the surface, forgiveness appears to be an act of graciousness toward another—releasing someone who has harmed you from blame and punishment. And indeed forgiveness does offer a second chance and new life to the one forgiven. But forgiveness also carries a secret benefit that is not obvious until you begin to practice it regularly. As the quote above says, when you forgive you discover that the person held captive by your anger and resentment is actually YOU.

When things fall apart in our lives it is normal to react with anger and sadness and to blame whoever or whatever we believe has caused our pain. We have a choice in that moment to step back and release the other person from our blame or to hold onto our negative emotions, but most of us have not developed the capacity to forgive so quickly. So we choose to hold onto blame, and each time we do that, we commit a bit of our life energy to the maintenance and storage of a negative memory.

Ultimately layers of resentment can form in our subconscious as we hold onto each and every slight or wound that has occurred in the past. Our subconscious mind can be filled with these old tangled, negative memories that can explode when we least expect it, like land mines, as we try to relate to other people. All it takes is a situation somewhat similar to the negative memory and our old stored emotion can be released in a fit of rage that seems out of proportion and out of our control, causing harm to our relationships.

These "explosions" of negativity are one of the emotional consequences of storing up old resentments, but our physical bodies can suffer as well. Lack of forgiveness can cause a state of chronic stress, which has been linked to high blood pressure, heart disease, and decreased immune function.[2]

But when we do practice forgiveness and release others from our anger, we actually "untangle" some of the knotted memories in the subconscious and set free the energy that had been devoted to maintaining them.[3] Genuine forgiveness becomes a powerful "medicine" that can heal both the receiver and the giver—physically, emotionally and spiritually —particularly when it is practiced regularly and for the good of all.[4]

Clearly, Forgiveness is one of the most important lessons you will struggle with on this inward journey from ego to Soul. You have everything to gain from learning how to see your enemies and their suffering with new eyes. But this task is not easily accomplished and you will face many challenges and pitfalls as you work your way through the painful memories you have been storing and maintaining for years.

DETOURS ALONG THE ROAD

Once you begin to intentionally practice the act of Forgiveness you will become aware of many obstacles within you that can interfere with your progress. Sometimes these obstacles turn into detours that can take you off the path of forgiveness altogether and distract you with distorted ways of thinking and uncontrolled emotions. Here are some of the common detours that can interfere with your growth toward practicing complete forgiveness:

Falling into **victim mode** is one of the detours that can sabotage your spiritual growth during this third lesson of the inward journey. If you have been severely traumatized or deeply wounded by another person, there is a necessary time for healing and consolation that follows the injury when it is appropriate to view yourself as a victim and be treated gently by others who validate your victimization. However it is possible to get trapped in this "victim mode" and to begin to identify yourself as a victim in other situations, as well. When this occurs there is usually some secondary gain from being cared for and sheltered by others: a certain amount of power can be derived from the role of a victim because others are afraid of adding to your trauma and will acquiesce to you rather than stand up to you.

In addition, perpetually playing the role of the victim allows you to abdicate responsibility for your own life and your behavior, because there is always someone else to blame who did something far worse than you have done. The victim mode fosters spiritual laziness and allows you to get by in life without facing the difficult task of forgiveness. For most people it is extremely challenging to move from victim to forgiver because all the power afforded by the victim role has to be surrendered and the self-pity it encourages must be dropped before growth can occur.

On this quest to learn the lesson of Forgiveness, another detour that can trap you is a sense of **entitlement**, believing that life owes you something because of your suffering. This detour keeps you stuck in the mindset that you should receive special treatment or allowances because you have experienced more pain than others—you are entitled to bypass the rules and regulations of life because you are more special than everyone else. If this attitude is successful for you and you actually convince others that you are entitled to favors, then this detour will be very hard to grow beyond and you may remain stuck there for years. The lure of easy acknowledgment and status is far too powerful for most of us to let go of while we learn to forgive.

Another detour that occurs while learning to forgive is caused by the Shadow passion of **vindictiveness**. Within our lowest selves, we can be unable to let go of hatred toward another who has caused us pain because we are caught in the trap of a deep desire for revenge. We may believe that it is only fair that the perpetrator be punished and hurt to the same degree that we were harmed and we can become addicted to our own thirst for revenge. Such a negative desire can boil up from our hidden Shadow and override our good intentions, obscuring from our vision the need for forgiveness.

In this case we can simmer for years in our anger, plotting scenarios that would allow us to "get even" with the other person and bring them down. Any positive event experienced by the other person adds more fuel to our lust for revenge and keeps us even more deeply stuck in this deadly detour. This is when the damaging consequences of unforgiveness occur— when the heart is twisted and stifled with deep anger and hatred. Finding the way back to the path of Forgiveness is the only solution to this destructiveness, but it is a challenging task that will require tremendous effort. If you are caught in such a detour right now you must begin to work on your "Forgiveness tools" to help you increase your ability to let go of vindictiveness.

THE EGO AND FORGIVENESS

To the lower mind and the ego, forgiveness is a preposterous idea that makes no sense whatsoever in this cause-and-effect world of the Garden. Retribution, revenge, anger and blame all seem to be sensible consequences for one's actions and there is no justifiable reason to allow a perpetrator to escape from rightful punishment. Indeed our legal system operates on this very logic, as those who are found guilty of violating the law are expected to pay the price. In our country's foreign policy, as well, there is an expectation that any harm done by another nation must be answered with equal if not greater force.

Since the primary function of the ego is protection, it makes sense that to the ego forgiveness means that you will be letting down your carefully constructed barriers of defense to a person who has already done you harm in the past. This seems a very risky and ill-advised choice to the ego: why would you let someone go free who has clearly done the wrong thing and will probably do it again? No wonder the lower self holds out for vindictive behavior and the victim role—forgiveness is not a viable alternative to the ego.

The only time the ego can be coaxed to consider forgiveness is when there is clear evidence that forgiveness is healthier for the self than holding onto resentment. Eventually the lower self can be persuaded to try forgiveness for selfish reasons, even though one study showed that self-motivated forgiveness is not as effective or as helpful to health as forgiveness that arises from compassion toward others. But to forgive at all, for any reason, is better than harboring hatred and resentment. Sometimes this ego-motivated version of forgiveness is the first step in a better direction and can lead eventually to more loving and Soul-centered releasing of anger in the future. Any step along the path is better than none, so we must start wherever we are and learn as much as we can in each moment and each situation. Moving toward forgiveness is a good thing no matter where or how it begins.

TRAVEL ADVISORY

As mentioned in the previous section, it is possible for the ego to accept the idea of forgiveness when it is being offered for selfish gain. When carried to an extreme there is a risk that the ego can masquerade as a forgiver in order to appear more virtuous than other people. Remember that the ego can derail the spiritual growth process by convincing you that egoic behavior really is spiritual and arising from your Soul. But in reality the ego is promoting itself as a martyr and feigning forgiveness as a means of gaining control over the growth process.

You can recognize the familiar signs of the ego if an offering of forgiveness is clothed in dramatic stories of the horrible wound that has occurred and the remarkable, self-less acts of (fake) forgiveness that have been performed. If you feel a sense of pride about your ability to forgive and find yourself using it to prove to others how spiritual you are, you may want to search for the presence of ego. An act of genuine forgiveness is best performed with an attitude of humility and in relative secret. Be sure to learn well the tricks of the ego and remember to be always watchful for little signs of false guidance along this journey. Keep your eyes open at all times for the deceit that might lead you astray.

THE SOUL AND FORGIVENESS

"The fault is in the blamer.
Spirit sees nothing to criticize."

-RUMI

The True Self or Soul actually has little need to practice Forgiveness because the Soul doesn't store up resentments. To the Soul there is no right or wrong, bad or good—everything that happens is just another learning experience here on planet Earth. So the Soul doesn't respond with judgment, anger or blame when something happens that wasn't desired or when another person behaves in a hurtful manner. The ups and downs of life are received as prime opportunities to learn and become an even more effective channel for Love and the Soul "sees nothing to criticize" as stated in the Rumi quote above.

From the Galaxy perspective, every action sets in motion forces that will lead to consequences. Those who choose to bring harm to others, for whatever reason, will create energy disturbances around themselves that will eventually be returned in one way or another and allow opportunities for learning to occur.

The Soul doesn't need to seek punishment of another because life itself will bring others all the lessons they need on their own journeys and paths. The Soul focuses only on its own path of growth and evolution by asking, "What can be learned from this?" And the Soul takes responsibility for choices made and actions taken, sometimes by seeking to repair damage that has been done to others.

For the Soul there is no real enemy, no one to blame, no one to hate ... there are only other souls on their own unique journeys, struggling to survive and learn from life as they go, suffering at times and needing all the love they can garner to help them along the path.

TRANSFORMING YOUR LIFE

At this point in your journey you have no doubt been betrayed, abandoned, hated, neglected, and harmed by many people in your life, including people who have supposedly loved you. No doubt you have felt hatred toward others and toward yourself as you've gone through the ups and downs of life. Now is the time to cultivate *mercy*: a compassionate understanding that everyone has been hurt and broken by life; everyone has fallen short of being their best selves; everyone has missed the mark.

Practicing mercy allows you to open your heart to those who have done harm while also holding them accountable for their actions. View your own "mistakes" in life with this same gift of mercy; you can love yourself inspite of your past behaviors and you can take responsibility to heal the wounds you've caused by making amends and restoring wholeness.

Use rituals and forgiveness practices to work through your own Shadow first and then turn to those "unforgivable" people in your life. Find mercy in your heart to release your resentment toward them even if your relationship with them can never be healed. Any act of forgiveness sets in motion a wave of healing energy that will ultimately lessen your pain and reduce the collective suffering of humanity.

TOOLS FOR THE JOURNEY

Forgiveness is a task that must be intentionally practiced and developed throughout life because it does not happen on its own. But it is one of the most important skills you will ever master. Forgiveness broadens and deepens your capacity for bringing *fearless love* to the planet and can accelerate the process of spiritual growth on your own inward journey. Visualize your bitterness and resentment toward others as threads of connection that have become knotted and tangled through hurtful experiences in the past. Those many knots and tangles have accumulated within and now prevent the free flow of love and compassion through you to others. Forgiveness is simply the process of loosening the knots one at a time. Much like untangling Christmas lights that have become a jumbled ball of wires and bulbs, it can take time and patience to work through the mass of twisted and confusing emotions stored deep inside of you. Though the task of forgiveness can seem overwhelming, remember that each knot you release will open a new channel for love and provide you with even more energy for your ongoing work of forgiveness. As you begin to carry and share more *fearless love* the burden of hatred on the planet is lessened and healing is fostered. Check the **Resources** page for these and other tools at www.eoluniversity.com/resources.

Mindset Shift

The Mindset Shift necessary to begin your forgiveness practice involves reframing the events of the past as experiences on your inward journey that can help you grow. Recognize that life is a classroom where you are continually presented with opportunities to learn new things and learning usually comes to us, like it or not, through difficulties. This shift in thinking happens gradually over time, layer-by-layer, so begin by thinking about smaller events that come to mind that you still feel some resentment over, perhaps residual anger toward a driver who stole the parking spot you had been waiting for or a neighbor whose loud party kept you awake one night. Consider these questions and write about them in your journal:

- What can I learn from the current or a past situation?
- How might I see this event from a broader perspective?
- What if no one is to blame and things just are the way they are?

Shadow Work:

Review your **Life Journey Map** and make note of any significant events from your past that still cause you pain, that still need your forgiveness. Now explore each of those events in your journal using the 3 steps of Shadow work:

1. Recognize: Where have I resisted forgiving other people or myself for hurtful behavior? Are there patterns to these experiences—do I tend to repeat the same circumstances over and over again?

2. Recover: How can I let go of my anger enough to stop seeking revenge against those who have hurt me? Where can I find room in my heart for peace instead of rage over the events of the past?

3. Rise above: What can I do differently when I see myself getting caught up in the same painful pattern? How can I love my wounded self more instead of blaming myself for the pain of my past?

Example: *After my father's death I experienced bitter anger and blame toward my mother, which was really a projection of my own feelings of guilt for his death. Over time I began to see that everything I felt toward her was actually what I was feeling about myself. When I faced my own guilt and shame I was able to work through it and forgive myself; then suddenly I no longer blamed my mother. As a result we were able to sit down together and share our mutual pain over his death, finally healing years of misunderstanding.*

PRACTICE

Techniques like **Ho'oponopono** and the **4-View Forgiveness Process** which you will find on the **Resource**

Page are recommended Practices to help you learn to forgive. Forgiveness must become part of your daily routine because it requires intention and dedication to actually achieve forgiveness. The human brain is wired to hold onto negative memories more tightly than positive memories as a means of protection from danger. Researchers estimate that up to 10 positive experiences are necessary in order to neutralize one negative memory, so to reach a state of forgiveness you have to consciously work on bringing light and love to your old wounds each day. At the end of the day look back at your experiences to see if there is anything you need to release so that it doesn't get stored as resentment. Choose to let go of whatever negative feelings you are holding and focus on gratitude instead. Be grateful for life, for the variety of experiences life brings you, and for the opportunity to grow and learn.

Polishing the Window is a helpful imagery practice to use while you work on this lesson. Remember that your view of the world around you and of your experiences within that world is influenced by the "window" or lens through which you look outside of yourself. Imagine that you are trying to view an outdoor garden through a dirty, foggy window. You can see outlines of shapes and some movement but everything is grey in color and not at all clear. In order to appreciate the true beauty of the garden you will need to polish the window to see through it without distortion. Recognize that your Shadow issues form the dirt and fog that alter the view through your window. As you do your Shadow work, you are cleaning the window, a little at a time, so that you can see other people and the events around you more clearly and truthfully.

Finally, you can utilize **Embracing the Enemy Within** as a simple practice to help you in your daily life. Whenever you identify an "enemy" outside yourself—someone who annoys you or arouses your anger—remember that this external "enemy" is a reflection of your own inner Shadow. Take a deep breath and as you inhale think: "You are not my enemy;" and as you exhale: "You are me." Later you can repeat this exercise in your mind by visualizing the other person and repeating the mantras. Imagine yourself gradually moving toward the other person until you can embrace them with both arms.

ACTION STEP

As an Action Step for forgiveness write a **Letter of Apology** to someone you have harmed. It isn't necessary to actually give the letter to the other person but you can do that if you choose. In the letter express your remorse without making excuses or justifying your behavior. Asked to be released from blame over the incident.

Next write a **Letter of Forgiveness** to someone who has harmed you that you feel ready to release from your anger and resentment. Explain that you can see the past differently now and you choose to no longer carry negative feelings. Again you don't need to actually send the letter because you will benefit from simply writing these words.

Finally when you feel satisfied that you have written these two letters from your highest self and you are ready to let go of shame for your own behavior and blame for the actions of the other person, use a candle flame or other form of fire to burn the letters. Watch as the paper is reduced to ash and envision your anger, guilt and remorse disintegrating as well.

6. THE FOURTH LESSON: THE PRESENT MOMENT

"Around us life bursts with miracles—a glass of water, a
  ray of sunshine, a leaf, a caterpillar, a flower,
  laughter, raindrops.
If you live in awareness, it is easy to see miracles
  everywhere."

-THICH NHAT HAHN

A s we begin the fourth lesson of the inward journey, we are reminded of the importance of living in awareness, in this Present Moment. The problem is that when everything falls apart we are challenged to keep our focus on the present because we feel our emotions so deeply in this moment. We are tempted to escape the current pain by focusing our thoughts in the past or future where emotions are numbed and easier to manage. But healing can only happen in the Present Moment, along with joy, love, and miracles. In fact, those who consistently dwell in the Present Moment, even when they are in pain, begin to recognize that *everything* is a miracle. Within the Present Moment, even the most ordinary and mundane aspects of life reveal the miraculous creative force that is the core of their existence. Thus the Present Moment is actually the Heaven on Earth that we long for; we can find *paradise* only in this moment, right here, right now.

THE CLINIC OF LITTLE MIRACLES

As I continued to carry out the Love Project in secret I began to recognize that certain events were taking place in the clinic I could only describe as "little miracles." This concept was not new to me as I had been introduced to the possibility of miracles at a very young age. According to my mother I nearly died when I was 5-years old and was "miraculously" resuscitated by EMT's in the back of an ambulance. A few years later I awakened in the middle of the night to see a beautiful translucent woman hovering over my bed and gazing down at me with pure love. I knew instantly that she was my Guardian Angel and would watch over me for all of my life. From that vision, along with my mother's stories, I began to see miracles all around me and to believe that life offers us these extraordinary experiences to guide and uplift us on our inward journeys through the darkness.

However my medical training, which focused solely on rational science, significantly challenged my old belief in miracles. None of my teachers or fellow students seemed to share that awareness so I found it necessary to set my perspective aside as I worked to master anatomy, physiology, pharmacology, and pathology in my quest to become the best doctor possible. But many years later, the little two-room shelter clinic gave me an opportunity to reconsider my appreci-ation for the miraculous and open my heart and mind, once again, to what is possible when we simply show up in the present moment.

The first time I ever used the word "miracle" in that clinic happened several months after we started seeing patients when a physician approached me at a monthly medical staff meeting for our local hospital. He handed me an old-fashioned kit for removing wax from the ear canal, containing a large steel syringe and several different tips to fit various-sized ears. He said he found it in the back of a closet, where it had been stored away after he upgraded to more modern equipment, and he wondered if I could use it for the shelter clinic. That very day I took the kit with me to the little clinic and—to my surprise—my first patient of the day came in with a large amount of wax impacted in both ear canals. Her hearing had been muffled for months because of the wax and she hadn't known what to do about it, but I had exactly the tool I needed to help her. I recognized in that moment that somehow things always seemed to work out well for us in that clinic. We always managed to get just enough to do what was needed for our patients.

When Charlotte expressed surprise over the perfect timing of the doctor's donation I remarked to her, "It's a little miracle!"

Charlotte, with her usual abrasiveness, frowned and replied, "It's a coincidence!"

By then I had already opened my heart and mind to the Love Project so it was an easy step for me to begin finding miracles everywhere I looked. But many months would pass before my skeptical assistant Charlotte could also see the little miracles that were happening all around us in that clinic. The turning point for her happened when we received a large plastic trash bag full of donated items from an unknown benefactor. At that time it was a regular occurrence for doctors or their staff members to drop off donations for us, so we frequently arrived at the little shelter clinic on Wednesdays to find random bags and boxes of supplies awaiting our inspection.

On this particular afternoon, Charlotte was sorting through the contents of the bag, which had been left at the clinic that morning, to see if there was anything that could be of use to us. She pulled out a frayed blanket and two stained pillows, then several tattered and filthy teddy bears, and finally a pair of Dr. Scholl's shoe inserts.

She threw the bag down with disgust and said, "We can't use any of this! Some people just clean out their closets and donate all their trash to us."

Absentmindedly, without looking up from the chart I was completing, I responded "Just leave the bag in the back of the closet and I'll take it to the Thrift Store on my way home."

But the groundwork had been laid for Charlotte to experience her first "little miracle" a few weeks later. On that day a young woman who had been staying in the shelter came to see us with a concern. She had just been hired as a waitress at a local restaurant—a job that would allow her to become independent and leave her abusive marriage. She was very excited about this opportunity but told us that after her first day of work her feet were aching badly from standing on them all day. She had experienced the same pain in the past due to fallen arches and she mentioned that the symptoms had been alleviated before by wearing arch supports in her shoes.

I glanced at Charlotte and could see that she had the same thought as me as she scampered off to the storage closet. She returned with the Dr. Scholl's shoe inserts that were still in the garbage bag I had somehow forgotten to take to the Thrift Store. Of course, the shoe inserts were exactly the size the young woman needed—they fit her shoes perfectly and her feet felt better instantly. As she thanked us and walked out the door with a huge smile on her face, Charlotte stood there with a bewildered look.

"It's a little miracle, Charlotte," I said.

She shook her head in agreement and whispered, "I know."

From that moment on, the miracles began to occur on a regular basis. We would receive some random item as a donation and within a week or so a patient would appear who needed that very thing. This happened frequently with medications and also with certain supplies, like casting materials or orthopedic supports for sprains and injuries. Whatever we needed in order to offer the best care seemed to arrive in our little shelter clinic just before the patient came in for an appointment.

Once someone donated an air splint made for the right ankle and sure enough a patient showed up one week later with a sprained right ankle. On another day a woman came in who needed a special cream for eczema that was very expensive. I knew that we didn't have any samples of the cream in the storage closet and I was certain that no one would donate such a costly medication to us. I had already told her we wouldn't be able to get that particular cream for her because the cost of a prescription would use up our entire annual budget of $200!

But then I remembered that there was a box of donated samples that I hadn't had time to go through yet, though I was still certain that I wouldn't find the medication there. However, when I opened the box I discovered that on the very top there was a small bag with sample tubes of the exact cream she needed. I was astonished and humbled once again by the precision with which we were being watched over in the little two-room shelter clinic—it was as if everything was being arranged somehow by some unseen force.

One day I saw a patient with extremely heavy menstrual bleeding that had been going on for days. I knew that she needed treatment right away because she had already lost a great deal of blood, so I called a local gynecologist to see if he would be willing to help her. He saw her in his office that same day, admitted her to the hospital and performed surgery later that night. Not only did he offer his services to her for free, he convinced the hospital and the anesthesiologist to write off their bills, as well. When I called to express my gratitude for his help he told me that giving free care to our patient had reminded him why he had chosen to become a doctor in the first place so many years before. He invited me to send him any patients from the shelter clinic who needed a gynecological consult but couldn't afford to pay. Over the next few years I sent him two more patients and again he thanked me for the opportunity to be of service. The little miracles seemed to be extending outside our clinic walls and were bringing transformation to others in our medical community, as well.

After several months, I noticed that Charlotte, my former skeptical partner, was now getting on-board with these miraculous occurrences.

One day when we received a box full of medication for shingles she told me, "Someone's going to be coming in with shingles in the next few weeks—we just got their medication in today."

Sure enough, a patient did arrive with shingles and we had exactly the right amount of medication for her. I smiled when I overheard Charlotte reassuring that patient, "Don't worry! We have just what you need here."

In perhaps the greatest miracle of all, Charlotte's demeanor had gradually transformed throughout these months we had worked together in our clinic of little miracles. She smiled more frequently, was often gentle and compassionate toward patients, and seemed to be enjoying her time in the clinic more than ever. Charlotte was becoming the teammate I had wished for—someone who could appreciate the Love Project and celebrate with me all the little miracles that were happening each week. And the most amazing part of all was that Charlotte and I didn't have to plan and struggle to create change for our patients. In fact, the most important task for each of us was just to show up every Wednesday afternoon in that little two-room shelter clinic and be fully present in each moment, with hearts full of love, and awareness that everything is indeed … a miracle.

As this story unfolded throughout the years I spent working in the shelter clinic I had the opportunity over and over again to confront my rational ego/mind that clung to science as the ultimate wisdom of life. In addition I struggled with my identity as a member of a profession that rejected spirituality and the idea of "miracles" altogether. I was being exposed to an aspect of healing through both my work in hospice and in the shelter clinic that I feared my colleagues would judge as unscientific and unprofessional. I was reluctant to share what I had witnessed in my work with other medical practitioners, including Charlotte, for fear of being rejected and expelled from my chosen career.

Some of my fear arose from my experience in residency when Christine the ER nurse had tried to have me kicked out of the training program. While I had forgiven Christine for her behavior I was still left with scars from the past that were an obstacle to being fully in the present moment. Each "little miracle" that I experienced at the shelter clinic served to pull me further away from the fear of the past toward the beauty and magnificence of the Present Moment. Gradually my ego was being asked to let go of that fear and relax into the *fearless love* that is possible when we dwell in the moment—right here, right now. And even Charlotte had begun to experience the transformative power of the "little miracles."

THE PATH OF THE PRESENT MOMENT

*"Don't despise the little steps you know you can take
     every day.
There are tiny miracles in each and every one of them."*

-ISRAELMORE AYIVORE

In *7 Lessons for Living from the Dying* we learned that dwelling in the Present Moment is the key to Paradise ... to living a life of miracles. It's important to note here that the word *paradise* does not refer to some perfect utopia where all of our wants and desires are met. But paradise describes a state of being "in the flow" of life with all of its ups and downs, losses and gains, and being able to see the hand of the Divine in everything that happens, including when things fall apart. Patients at the very end of their lives are thrust into the present moment because they no longer have a future to project themselves into and the past becomes less relevant in the face of dying. Many of those terminal patients, as shown in the stories from that book, learn to savor each and every breath of life because they recognize that they have only a few precious moments remaining. This awareness of the fleeting nature of life and the ability to appreciate the present moment is actually one of the profound gifts of the dying process.

But the rest of us, who are not currently facing a terminal diagnosis, are less aware of the finiteness of life in physical form and must learn how and why to keep our attention focused on the present moment. Many of us exist for the most part in the past, continuously recycling and rehashing old memories, usually about negative experiences. Or we spend our time and life energy worrying and dreaming about the future—projecting ourselves into events and situations that have not happened and may never occur. Our minds generally require training, such as mindfulness meditation, in order to stay focused on what is happening right here, right now in this very moment.

Much of our contemporary entertainment, like movies, television programs, and video games, keep our minds engaged in fantasy and help us ignore the reality of the present moment. In some ways as a society we are addicted to functioning outside of the present and have become attached to the familiarity of the past or the fantasy of the future. Illness, tragedy, trauma, dying, and other situations when life falls apart are events that can wake us up to experience the here and now as they initiate our inward journeys. Occasions of extreme joy, such as a wedding or the birth of a child, can also jolt us into the present moment, but unfortunately they tend to be short-lived encounters with the *Now* that easily become overwhelmed with the concerns of past and future.

In an earlier story, I was propelled into the present moment in my teens by the death of my classmate, which awakened me to the reality that I too will one day die. Many years later my father's death and the grief that ensued also brought me continually back to the present moment as I suffered with emotional pain and guilt for several years. Traumatic experiences such as these allow us to see a glimpse of the *Now* through the lens of pain and remind us that this moment, right here, right now, is the only thing that is real. But without training, our minds will easily slip back into reverie for the past or the future.

While the task of remaining focused on the present moment at all times is daunting and nearly impossible to fulfill, being present in certain situations is much more achievable. As in the story above, with practice I became able to bring my full presence to each patient encounter at the little shelter clinic for a few hours each week. During those office visits I learned to leave my past and future concerns behind while I focused on the needs of the patient, and particularly on bringing love to each present moment. This practice gradually brought harmony and peace to the entire clinic, to the patients, to Charlotte, and to the rest of my life, as well.

The possibility of miracles occurring became more likely when energy was brought to the present moment and not squandered on past or future worries. For me and eventually for Charlotte, those synchronicities that happened on a regular basis in the clinic were indeed miracles. We had *what* was needed exactly *when* it was needed. This was the corollary lesson taught in 7 *Lessons for Living from the Dying*, as well: in Paradise, you will have what you need, with the reminder that "what you *want* may not be the same as what you *need*."

THE WISDOM OF THE PRESENT MOMENT

> *This silence, this moment, every moment,*
> *if it's genuinely inside you,*
> *brings what you need.*

-RUMI

Life can only truly be lived in the present moment. If we are unable to bring our energy and attention to this very moment, then it will be lost to us ... as well as the next moment and the next. However, if we have learned to master the previous lesson of Forgiveness we will suddenly find that a renewed supply of life force energy has become available for spending in the Present Moment. As mentioned in the last chapter, the act of forgiveness frees up the energy that we have been squandering on the maintenance of old resentments and entanglements. When they are released that energy becomes available for our use and for fueling creativity and synchronicities ... or little miracles ... in this present moment.

Each of the wisdom traditions teaches us a similar message, that we should live only in this moment. Sri Nisargadatta Maharaj reminded his followers: "Past and future are in the mind only—I am now." When our minds become obsessed with the past and future we are unable to live in this present moment and the miracles of healing and creativity become unavailable to us.

Buddha attributed our very wellbeing to the practice of living in the present: "The secret of health for both mind and body is not to mourn for the past, worry about the future or anticipate troubles, but to live in the present moment wisely and earnestly." The energy available to us in the present moment after releasing past resentments helps our bodies and minds restore and maintain health.

In the New Testament we are reminded of the fleeting nature of life itself: "How do you know what your life will be like tomorrow? Your life is like the morning fog—it's here a little while, then it's gone." (James 4: 14, NLT) For this same reason the Torah advises us to celebrate each and every day: "This is the day the Lord has made; we shall exult and rejoice thereon." (Tehillim 118:24)

While you can learn the wisdom of the Present Moment by studying these traditions and the writings of their sages, you must develop your own practice over a great deal of time in order to actually bring your focus and attention to each and every moment.

Setting the *intention* to be present in this moment is the first and most important step you can take.

From that beginning you can return over and over again to the delicate balance of the present. Each time you find yourself caught up in the past or future you can start over again in this moment, bringing your attention to right here, right now.

By practicing in this way, no matter how frustrating or slow the process seems, you gradually train your mind to notice what is right in front of you and to begin to set aside its obsessive thoughts of past and future. You will find surprising serenity within the present moment as you breathe and relax in the here and now. All possibility, all creativity and all miracles are available to you in this very moment.

However, I recently spoke with a woman who is grieving the death of her mother. She said that everyone tells her that if she stays in the present moment she will always be happy. But in the midst of her grief she feels totally present and also totally sad. This is an excellent reminder that the present moment is filled with whatever we are experiencing in that moment. Sadness is a feeling not to be repressed or ignored but to be embraced when it occurs. To live authentically we must be capable of experiencing the full range of emotions within each and every present moment.

DETOURS ALONG THE ROAD

> *Most humans are never fully present in the now, because*
> *unconsciously they believe that the next moment*
> *must be more important than this one.*
> *But then you miss your whole life, which is never*
> *not now.*

-ECKHART TOLLE

As you work to live your life fully in each and every moment there are several detours that can divert your course and take you away from the path that lies in front of you. As mentioned before, while these side roads can appear to be obstacles or hindrances to your growth, they usually end up leading you exactly where you need to go, to learn something that could only be taught by that particular situation. So remember to embrace all the turns and unexpected forks on your winding path and approach them with curiosity and a willingness to mine them for whatever treasures they have to offer.

Grief, which was already mentioned as a detour on the path of Suffering, is also one of the most common side roads on the quest to dwell in the Present Moment. Our pain and sadness over the loss of a loved one can keep us trapped in the past for many years, if we focus on old memories instead of experiencing the feeling of sadness in this moment. That is what happened with my own grief after the death of my father when I was trapped waiting for things to return to the way they were before he died. The breaking of our hearts through physical separation from those we love can be so intense that we retreat into our memory as the only place of solace. Constantly reviewing what has happened in the past, reliving old experiences, and even rewriting our memories to make them more pleasing can provide us with brief escapes from the acute pain of loss.

Consulting with psychics and mediums to stay in communication with our loved ones can be an effective tactic for surviving the suffering of our grief but can also become a detour. Any coping mechanisms that help us live through grief in a positive way are an acceptable part of the journey. However at some point they can fail to serve us if they distract us for too long from the present moment, which is where healing and growth can occur. Learning to live with grief is an important part of our inward journey that ultimately must lead us back to the miracle of the present.

The next detour from the path of the Present Moment to be examined is that of **hopefulness**. We tend to view hope as a positive and desirable quality and equate it with our ability to survive difficult situations like loss and illness. And while it can be helpful to have an optimistic outlook on life, being in a state of hopefulness actually propels us into the future, as we anticipate, desire and yearn for things to be different than they are right here, right now in the present moment.

One of the most subtle and harmful applications of hopefulness occurs within the medical profession. Doctors frequently offer "hope" to their patients in the form of a lengthy or uncomfortable treatment process that may or may not result in a cure. They are unaware that while they encourage their patients to "keep hoping" they are actually guiding them to focus on the future and making it more difficult for them to be fully in the present moment, which is where love, miracles and healing exist.

On many occasions I experienced my colleagues reluctantly referring their patients to our hospice after they had run out of treatment options, and expressing regret that there was no more hope for them. But the loss of this "hopefulness," which is actually a false focus on a future that does not yet exist, was the best thing that could have happened for those patients. Finally when they could stop investing their energy in hope for a future cure, they could bring their attention to the present and begin to live fully in each and every moment. Some of those patients actually improved and lived much longer than expected, many found true comfort and deep meaning by living fully in the moment during their final days, and a few, as described in 7 *Lessons for Living from the Dying*, experienced healings that were truly miraculous.

We can easily be swept away from the present moment and into this state of longing for a different future by a variety of life situations. In the midst of a "hopefulness" detour we can believe that we have the best attitude and outlook possible for our current difficult circumstances. The lure of "hope" and its magnetic pull on us toward the future can be subtle and can go unrecognized for a very long time. But the wisdom of the present moment teaches us that instead of looking to the future to bring the positive answer we desire, we must instead learn to see this moment, right here, right now, as perfect: full of possibility and meaning, and also empty of expectation and desire.

There is nothing more than this moment. You have everything you need right here, right now. Focus on *Now* to maximize your comfort, peace, love, and wellbeing. This is the profound lesson the Present Moment brings to us as it guides us gradually, through the perils of illness, loss and devastation, on this inward journey of our earthly existence.

THE EGO AND THE PRESENT MOMENT

The ego struggles to be at peace in the Present Moment because it can only see itself through the lens of the past or the future. Conjuring up memories of the past, whether truthful or distorted, allows the ego to create a favorable context for its own existence. Through the murky looking glass of memory, past accomplishments can be aggrandized while any failures can be blamed on someone or something else. Focusing on "who I think I was" is easier than determining "who I am" and the ego is comfortable keeping its gaze on the positive aspects of the past. In addition, the imagination can contrive vivid pictures of a future self that also can be more desirable than whatever exists in the here and now.

So the ego vacillates between past and future, always peering at a false reflection, holding on to the veil of illusion that obscures the Present Moment. Remember also that the tools of the ego are *fear* and *greed* so the ego will conjure up anxiety about the future and a perpetual sense of scarcity as it operates in the world. As an example, the authoritarian rulers we've discussed in other chapters keep their followers constantly off balance and out of the present moment by propagating false threats of danger and deprivation. These ego-driven leaders know how to control others by appealing to their lower selves and spreading chaos wherever they go.

The ego will be pulled into the past or the future over and over again as it struggles to learn how to balance in the here and now and not be swayed by its own fear and greed. To dwell solely in this present moment—trusting that it contains everything you need, expressing gratitude for what "is" rather than what was or will be, embracing the "little" birth and death contained in each breath—requires faith, and the ego alone cannot experience genuine faith without help from its long-lost friend, the Soul. As in the story that began this chapter, the ego —like the skeptical nurse Charlotte—will demand to be shown evidence over and over again that everything is perfect just as it is right now: there is nothing to strive or hope for; nothing to regret; and nothing to change in this very moment.

TRAVEL ADVISORY

As we have seen previously, it is important to be aware of the pitfalls that can sabotage or undermine each of the lessons on the inward journey. The ego, in its attempt to hijack the entire process of spiritual growth, is extremely skilled at appearing to be what it is not. Therefore we must be diligent about watching for the signs of ego as we travel this path.

During our struggle to dwell in the Present Moment the tricky ego actually poses a threat by lurking within the very practices we utilize to develop our capacity for presence. When the ego is secretly in charge, a spiritual journeyer can appear to be doing everything just right: meditating for long hours, listening to spiritual teachers, following the wisdom of ancient texts. But in fact, the act of "**seeking**" to grow spiritually has become a diversion away from "being" fully present in the moment. In these situations, the spiritual seeker is trying to do what an enlightened being would do and putting energy and attention into the "appearance" of enlightenment. But all of that effort and "doing" takes the seeker out of the present moment and into the illusion of spiritual achievement.

Genuine spiritual growth requires constant attention to the Shadow and work to heal or dissolve the internal obstacles that prevent the free flow of *fearless love* within.

The ego greatly fears the exposure that occurs whenever the Shadow is illuminated and explored and therefore seeks to avoid a confrontation with the dark side of the self. By engaging in overly-spiritual practices the ego can hide behind the outward behaviors of spirituality and pretend to be enlightened and comfortable in the present moment.

But in reality this constant seeking of growth is a ruse to prevent the actual work that would lead to genuine growth from taking place. The spiritual student who feels compelled to display his spiritual practices to others and to seek out praise for them has very likely been tricked by the ego into believing he has transcended the Shadow and mastered the ego. The wise student stays alert to the workings of ego at all times and becomes a master at spotting the ego in disguise.

THE SOUL AND THE PRESENT MOMENT

> *"On a day when the wind is perfect, the sail just needs to open and the world is full of such beauty. Today is such a day."*

> -RUMI

The Soul cares little about the past or future and dwells only in this Present Moment; so for the Soul there is no struggle to stay right here, right now. The Soul recognizes the infinite abundance of the Present Moment: that you will have what you need in each and every moment in order to learn and grow on this inward journey.

The Soul has no longing or desire for anything other than "what is"; no need to blame anyone or anything for the past, since the past no longer exists; and no concerns for the future because it has not yet happened. The Soul can witness this moment and see the perfection within it regardless of the actual details of the current situation. The Soul brings only *fearless love* to this Present Moment and urges you always to just open your sails—"the world is full of such beauty" and there are little miracles *everywhere.*

TRANSFORMING YOUR LIFE

Living fully in the Present Moment is a simple but difficult task. You are surrounded by distractions that constantly pull your attention away from what you are experiencing in the here and now. But learning how to return your focus to where you are and what you are doing right now is one of the greatest keys to getting through difficult times.

When the world seems to be on fire or overcome with violence and hatred you may find yourself overwhelmed with anxiety and hopelessness. But if you can stop for one second, take a deep breath and look around at where you are right now, you will find that in this moment you are all right. In fact, you might notice that there are rays of sunlight making a beautiful pattern on the ground, or that there is a lovely song playing on the radio, or that a tiny flower is blooming in the garden, or that the smell of freshly-brewed coffee is coming from the kitchen. These small delights of the Present Moment are the little building blocks of a meaningful and joyful life. Start right now, close your eyes and breathe deeply. You are here, you are alive, and in this moment you have everything you need.

TOOLS FOR THE JOURNEY

Learning to keep your attention and energy in the Present Moment takes practice and determination. When you decide to focus on the present you will begin to notice how frequently your thoughts are caught up in the past or future and how little you are engaged in this very moment. To develop your ability to be fully present you must dig deep into your own Shadow and let go of old resentments that trap your energy in the past, so you will need to master the previous lesson of Forgiveness before you can make progress in the lesson of Presence. Check the **Resources** page for these and other tools at www. eoluniversity.com/resources.

· · ·

MINDSET SHIFT

The Mindset Shift you will need in order to become more present is to see life as unfolding and changing in each and every moment. As you learn to let go of the past you also let go of whatever identity you held onto in the past and allow yourself to become a new person with each breath. Recognize that you used to view your life as a collection of events that have already occurred, but now you are asked to be more fluid and open to change so that life can reveal itself to you through one moment after another. And life is constantly revealing itself through the little experiences of the present—the sound of the wind outside your window, the smell of a freshly cut rose, the taste of a piece of fruit. The more you are able to connect to the present moment through your senses the more you are opening to joy, love and creativity, which all manifest in present time. Write in your journal:

- What am I experiencing with my 5 senses right now in this moment in time?
- What do I notice around me?
- What feelings are arising within me?
- What needs to be healed, either physically or emotionally, in this moment?

SHADOW WORK

Remember that *fear* and *greed* are the two Shadow tools of the ego that prevent you from appreciating the present moment. Review your **Life Journey Map** and find any instances where fear or greed played a role in your decision-making. Then write about them in your journal using the 3 steps of Shadow work:

1. Recognize: What circumstances trigger fear in me now? When do I tend to act out of greed rather than generosity? What traumatic experiences in the past may have taught me to react with fear or greed?

2. Recover: How can I find more safety and trust within myself? Where do I need to focus on loving myself more to counteract fear and greed?

3. Rise above: How can I remind myself to return to the present moment whenever fear arises? What practices will help me feel more whole and secure in my daily life?

Example: *In my medical practice my greatest fear was that I would in some way cause harm to a patient. At times the fear was so great that it would paralyze me and prevent me from making quick decisions. By working on my Shadow I was able to identify the fear as arising from a lack of love and trust for myself. As my self-love began to grow I utilized deep breathing to help me stay calm and make the best possible decisions in tense situations.*

PRACTICE

One of the best Practices for learning to stay in the Present Moment is **deep breathing,** because the breath always brings us back to the here and now. Start and end each day with a series of three deep breaths. Inhale slowly and envision that you are breathing in sparkling molecules of love. As you exhale long and slowly see these sparkles coursing through your entire body and replacing the stagnant energy of the past with vibrant light-filled molecules of the present moment. Deep breathing in this way will help you relax, lower your stress level, and improve your focus on what is happening right here, right now.

The **Resource Page** has a description of more breathing exercises.

If you like you can repeat this **Mantra for the Present Moment** while you practice deep breathing:

> I am here.
> I am now.
> I am love.
> We are here.
> We are now.
> We are love.
> There is only here.
> There is only now.
> There is only love.

Another simple practice to increase your ability to be present is **Contemplation of Beauty**. Look around you and notice beauty anywhere you can find it: a painting on the wall, a flower in your garden, the setting sun, a stone on the path, a bowl of fruit, the way water swirls as it travels down the drain. When you are fully present there is literally beauty everywhere, in everything. The more you can remind yourself to find beauty around you, the more you will be focusing on the present moment and creating peace within you.

ACTION STEP

Medical hypnotherapist Roger Moore[1] teaches his clients the mantra **"Right now I'm okay"** to emphasize that in this present moment, right here and right now, everything is actually fine. As your action step for this lesson, write this phrase on a piece of paper and post it on your wall or carry it in your wallet to remind you to get back to that place of equanimity in the present moment. Repeat these words whenever you feel you are being swept away by past regrets or worries about the future. Take a deep breath and recall that in this very moment there is nothing to fear.

7. THE FIFTH LESSON: PURPOSE

*"Our own life has to be our message. ...
If you touch one thing with deep awareness,
you touch everything."*

-THICH NHAT HAHN

As we continue on the inward journey to the fifth lesson, having mastered already the challenges of Suffering, Love, Forgiveness and the Present Moment, we must directly confront our need to live a life of Purpose. One of the goals we embrace for our modern life here on planet Earth is to recognize and delineate a specific reason or explanation for this existence. While we hope our lives have a special or lofty purpose, the words of Thich Nhat Hahn remind us of the true simplicity of the spiritual path. Life itself is the message we bring to mankind—there is no more profound Purpose than simply being alive, moment-to-moment. And if we do, at some time, manage to touch one thing, to make a differ-

ence to just one person, then we will have touched everything ...
we will have changed the world.

LIFE IS THE MESSAGE

*Things were going quite well in the two-room shelter clinic after Char-
lotte began to appreciate the little miracles that were occurring and to
find joy in the work we were doing together every Wednesday afternoon. But for some reason, not all was well with me. I had fallen into
a state of emotional despair and was feeling detached and exhausted
with my volunteer work at the shelter, as well as my work in hospice. I
understood that this feeling had something to do with my ongoing
struggle with grief over my Dad's suicide because the anniversary of
his death had recently passed.*

*But I couldn't seem to pull myself out of my darkness, so I
decided to take a little "time out" to rest and recover my enthusiasm
for the Love Project. I told Charlotte and the shelter director that I
would be away for two weeks and they decided to shut down our
little clinic while I was absent. I continued my hospice work during
those weeks but at least I would have two Wednesdays totally free to
do some inner work and explore what was troubling me.*

*On one of those free afternoons I took my dog for a hike up to a
lovely waterfall in a canyon not far from my home. I sat on a rock
where I could feel both the warmth of sunlight and the spray of
tumbling water on my skin. Taking in the beauty and solitude of my
surroundings I recognized that Dad also would have appreciated this
place, if I had ever had the opportunity to bring him there. As I felt the
familiar anguish of unmet dreams and desires that had weighed me
down since the day he took his life, a lingering question entered my
thoughts: Did the fact that Dad had chosen to end his life prematurely
mean that his life had been a failure?*

My heart ached as I allowed long-suppressed emotions of guilt, fear, doubt, and sorrow to come to the surface. Why hadn't Dad been able to find enough meaning in his own life to go on living? The uncertainty haunted me: Did he leave the planet without ever knowing why he was here? Why had he given up on his life purpose? And after I had the courage to verbalize those fears there were other disturbing questions that emerged: What about my own life—was I actually living my purpose or was I just pretending that life has meaning? Would I be tempted to give up one day too, just like my father?

I was revisiting the same fear that had overcome me when my friend Jolene died at age sixteen. What if life actually has no meaning or purpose? What if none of this matters at all? Perhaps for my entire life I had foolishly been trying to create meaning where there was none. I had to admit to myself that I was angry at Dad for shattering my comfortable belief system. He hadn't cared enough about his own life to protect it but he also hadn't cared enough to protect me. This was the source of deep anger I had been repressing for years. My father who I loved so much had abandoned me and I couldn't forgive him for that or forgive my own bitterness toward him.

As the falling water crashed against the rocks below I was flooded with conflicting emotions and drowning in my own unanswered questions. But from the depths of my despair an old memory began to take shape in my mind. This story took place many years before at another time in my life when I had questioned my purpose and wondered why I was here on this planet:

I had just graduated from college and was coping with the devastating news that I had not been accepted into any of the six medical schools to which I had applied. I was shocked and deeply wounded by this turn of events because I had been preparing to be a doctor since the age of 12: with 4 years of Latin in high school, a double-

major in biology and chemistry in college, and volunteer work at hospitals and clinics. I had done everything I was supposed to do to get into medical school, including graduating summa cum laude from college and scoring well on the MCAT test.

When I called each of the schools to find out why I had been rejected I was even more hurt to hear some of their reasons: I was from the wrong place ("We only accept in-state students"); I had the wrong parents ("We prefer students who have at least one doctor in the family"); and I was too spiritual ("We're uncomfortable that you feel being a doctor is your 'life purpose'").

Humiliated and seeing myself as a total failure, I returned home to do some post-graduate work at the University of Wyoming while I tried to figure out what to do with my life. I registered for a few classes, started a research project in the biochemistry lab on campus, and got a job as a bartender in the evenings to support myself.

For months I was despondent and too ashamed to tell anyone that I hadn't been accepted to medical school. I didn't think I could find the courage and energy to go through the application process again, especially when I felt so betrayed by my own belief that becoming a doctor was my purpose. If I was truly meant to be a doctor, I reasoned, I should have been accepted into medical school the first time I applied.

The message seemed to be that I had followed the wrong guidance for all those years when I was preparing myself for a career in medicine. Confused and wounded I was angry at God for allowing my dream to be crushed and also worried that I had failed everyone in my life who had believed in my goal to become a doctor.

My mother was visibly disappointed to learn that I was working as a bartender and questioned me: "I thought you wanted to heal people … but now you're serving them alcohol?"

I couldn't explain to her the depth of my shame and disillusionment that everything I had worked so hard to achieve had fallen apart. This was my struggle to bear all on my own.

*But time passed and despite my own discouragement, I gradu-
ally began to love my work as a bartender. The job provided ample
opportunities to observe people from all walks of life and I was fascinated by the many characters I met who happened to gather at that
particular bar sometime along their own unique paths. From the
lonely widower who came in for "just one drink," to the desperate
woman in the skimpy dress who went home with a different man each
night, to the traveling businessman who was preparing for an important meeting, to the construction workers who stopped off for a beer
at the end of each day: I loved to take in their stories, observe their
interactions, and study their ways of coping with life's ups and
downs.*

*I would later recognize that my listening skills were being sharp-
ened during those days as a bartender as I learned to see through the
outer façade to the True Self of each and every person. In fact,
though I didn't know it them, bartending had turned out to be the
perfect pre-requisite training for my eventual medical career.*

*One night a gentleman I had never seen before came in alone,
sat at the bar, and ordered a "Rye & 7." Business was slow that
night so as I poured the whiskey and 7-Up into a glass for him I
already knew I was going to hear his story. He told me he worked
full-time in an oilfield in Saudi Arabia and only came home to the
U.S. for a few weeks each year to maintain his citizenship. He didn't
own a home here or have any family members to visit so he would
just travel around and see new parts of the country each year during
his stay.*

*I immediately felt comfortable with him for some reason and we
struck up a conversation that lasted throughout the evening. We
talked about politics, philosophy, history and life while he drank his
Rye & 7 and I washed glasses behind the bar. I found myself
confiding in him that I hadn't gotten into medical school and had no
idea what to do with my life now.*

He reassured me "You'll apply again and you'll get in the next time. You've got your whole life to become a doctor. Don't even worry about it right now."

I was surprisingly comforted by his advice and felt grateful that he had come in on a slow night so that we had time for this conversation.

As he was finishing his last drink and I was getting ready to close the bar he said to me, "You know, I've had the darnedest feeling all night that I've met you before. You seem so familiar to me."

I was puzzled since I was sure there was no way our paths could have crossed in the past.

A moment later his face lit up with recognition: "I know what it is! You remind me of someone else I met a long time ago."

He went on to tell me about the last time he had driven through Wyoming, ten years earlier. He had stopped over in the town of Casper for the night and had gone to the bar at his hotel for a few drinks, just like this night. There he met a very interesting man who was also sitting alone at the bar. The two of them had talked for hours about politics, philosophy, history and life—just like the conversation he and I held on this evening, ten years later.

He told me that the man at the bar was the wisest person he had ever met and he had never forgotten the inspiration he took away from their discussion. Though the man he met was wearing greasy old coveralls and told him he just came from working at a gas station, the bartender later revealed that he was actually one of the owners of the hotel.

"I don't think I've ever met a greater man or one with so much humility." He added, "And that's who you remind me of."

My eyes filled with tears and my hands were shaking with emotion as I responded, "That man was my father. You met my father ten years ago."

Totally taken by surprise he plopped down onto the barstool again while he considered this revelation. "You look like him. You talk like him. You are the female version of him!"

I nodded in agreement, too stunned to speak. What were the odds that this man would meet both my father and me, ten years apart, in two different cities in Wyoming while traveling through on his way to somewhere else? At that moment standing behind the bar I fully understood that I was exactly where I was supposed to be right there, right then; and that everything was perfect, including not getting into medical school that year.

I knew that my Dad had been where he was supposed to be that night ten years earlier and that this traveling man's journey had twice taken him where he was meant to be as well. I stood there in awe for a moment at this epiphany and was aware of electricity coursing through my body.

When it was time for the stranger to leave neither of us was sure how to say goodbye. He stood up, tucked a wad of bills under his glass, and shook my hand, "My dear. This evening has been an honor and a privilege."

"Yes, for me too!" I waved as he walked away.

When he reached the door he turned and added, "You're going to be a fantastic doctor!"

Sitting by the waterfall so many years later after so much more history had unfolded, I looked back on the magic of that encounter: how my Dad had made such an impression on this man's life, how the same man had met me ten years later under similar circumstances, and how he had rekindled my belief that I could one day become a doctor. I understood in that moment that my Dad had fulfilled his purpose all throughout his life simply by living each day that he was here and by being who he was in every situation.

After Dad's death we had learned from numerous visitors to his gas station that he had quietly helped many people over the years: repairing their cars for free and filling their tanks with gas when they couldn't afford to pay. In one case he even bought groceries for a young couple with a baby who had been stranded on their way to a new job in a nearby town.

Even though he chose to end his own life it didn't diminish the meaning Dad had already created. I would never understand why he made the choice he did but my fear that his life had no purpose had subsided along with some of my anger toward him.

I also recognized that I too was living my own purpose, day-after-day, even though I felt broken and confused much of the time. I was reassured that my purpose for that moment was to continue working at the little two-room shelter clinic and to keep caring for patients in hospice. There was nothing more I needed to know. I just had to trust that my path would unfold before me when I least expected it.

I returned to the shelter clinic after my two-week break with a renewed commitment to be the best person I could be no matter how I was feeling. I would gather up the pieces of my broken heart once again and get back to work offering Love to every patient who walked through the door.

Charlotte was thrilled to see me back at the clinic and told me she had been working on a special project of her own during the two weeks I was away. She retrieved a large plastic bag from our storage closet and pulled from it the old Teddy bears that someone had donated many months before. But they looked entirely different: Charlotte had washed them, stitched up and patched their damaged places, sewn on new button eyes, and tied brightly colored ribbons around their necks.

"I rescued the bears!" she announced proudly. "Now we have something to give away to the kids who come to the clinic."

From that day on, Charlotte began collecting unwanted Teddy bears and spent hours at home refurbishing them as gifts for our young patients. Sometimes those bears ended up in the arms of older patients, as well, who needed something to hug and love during their lonely days at the shelter. Now Charlotte had found new *purpose for her own life in salvaging the battered old Teddy bears that, in turn, helped us salvage the lives of the battered and unwanted women and children in the shelter.*

The transformation I witnessed in Charlotte was miraculous: she now moved through each clinic day with joy as she helped me heal the broken hearts and patch up the wounded Souls who passed through our little two-room shelter clinic. And I was healing too as I settled back into my volunteer work every Wednesday afternoon. Side-by-side now Charlotte and I carried out The Love Project— touching one life at a time and changing everything in the process. But we had no idea what changes were awaiting our own lives just around the corner ...

In this story I was struggling with the perennial question of human existence: What am I doing here? The crisis of my Dad's suicide had clearly shifted my path to working in hospice and the shelter clinic, but I still wasn't sure that I was doing what I was " supposed to do." My ego had accepted the common belief that each life has one special purpose and that our task is to find that purpose and be devoted to it throughout our years. No wonder I feared that my Dad, who had owned and operated a gas station his entire adult life, might not have found his purpose—that he might have ended his life without accomplishing what he came here to do.

I had fallen into a trap that the ego creates for itself by believing in an unattainable goal that exists somewhere in the future and then suffering with despair when that goal is never reached. The memory of the man I met in the bar who had also met my father ten years earlier returned to me at just the right moment.

Both the synchronicity of that original event and then my

recollection of it while sitting by the waterfall came at times when I needed a reminder that life's purpose is not something that will happen in the future—it is unfolding for us moment-by-moment as we simply breathe and be our best selves. That message was so powerful that even Charlotte discovered it for herself during my time away from the clinic. Her Teddy bears became a symbol for me of finding purpose by simply being present in each and every moment, making the most of whatever life has given us, and being guided by *fearless love.*

THE PATH OF PURPOSE

On this inward journey of spiritual growth we now encounter the challenge of understanding our true Purpose, which was shown in 7 *Lessons for Living from the Dying* to be: "Manifest Your Highest Potential." Each of us must engage in an individual struggle to find our purpose in life and for some of us the search can occur at a point of crisis as in the story above. We have been taught that our life purpose is something we are working toward or striving to achieve, such as material wealth, a particular career, or other accomplishment.

Our entire process of formal education is geared toward this idea of purpose. You are expected to know "what you want to be when you grow up" at a young age and to begin preparing yourself for that path as you advance through the educational system. Elementary school is preparation for middle school, which gets you ready for high school, which opens the door to college, which is expected to lead either to further education or to the career that you have chosen to pursue. At each step along the way you are only fulfilling the tasks necessary to move you to the next step and the next step so that one day in the future you will finally be where you are meant to be and your life will make sense. And many of us never really identify our "purpose" or even if we have, later come to question the very choices we made earlier in life.

The problem here lies in our misunderstanding of the concept of Purpose. When we believe that there is one path we must find in order to fulfill our purpose, then we limit our life's choices to the possibilities we can imagine. And, as we have seen, many times that path we are trying to follow is elusive and obstructed. Then we can lapse into moments of despair as we question our entire existence and wonder if we are even capable of living up to our own expectations.

However in order to master the lesson of Purpose, it is necessary to throw out these old outdated ideas because they don't serve us well and can actually lead us astray. If we can come to recognize that each moment of life has its own potential and that when we live in the present moment we are manifesting that potential, then suddenly all of life consists of one moment after another of living our best life, of bringing our unique message to the world.

As I came to realize in the story, even my Dad's life, which ended unexpectedly with his suicide, manifested his potential during the moments that he was alive, simply because he was himself and brought his "message" to each and every moment. His life purpose was no more and no less than that: living each moment fully while he was alive.

THE WISDOM OF PURPOSE

"Yesterday I was clever, so I wanted to change the world. Today I am wise so I am changing myself."

-RUMI

Purpose is now a catchword commonly heard within the New Age Movement. There are many coaches, books, courses and workshops to help you discover your purpose so that you can begin living it now. We are captivated by the idea that we are here for a special reason and need only discover that reason in order to start living the life of our dreams. We fantasize that we will receive everything we want in life as soon as we figure out and begin fulfilling our one Divine Purpose. But I have encountered many disillusioned people on this journey who thought they were living their purpose only to discover that their lives actually fell apart, rather than falling into place and making sense to them.

Rumi points out that our "cleverness", which I interpret to mean our intellectual perspective on life, tells us that we should set out to change the world. After all, we can clearly see what's wrong with the current state of affairs, so it would be perfect if our purpose turned out to be "fixing the world" in some way or another. Many of us have invested a tremendous amount of time, energy and money into world-changing causes in support of our life's purpose. But change of this magnitude is difficult to accomplish and may not always result from the efforts of a single person, even though it is *possible* for that to happen. The trick is to understand when and how to apply your best energy to a cause outside of yourself, so that you can maximize the benefits from your investment.

But Rumi tells us that it is far better to be wise—and true wisdom points us toward digging deep and "fixing" what is wrong with ourselves before we set out to change the world. Each iota of energy that we invest in healing our own Shadow, letting go of resentments, and bringing more love into the world, creates change in the entire cosmos, without our understanding of how and why this happens. When we transform ourselves we set in motion the ripples of change that have an impact on everything else. So in Rumi's view of things, changing ourselves is our true purpose and deserves to be the focus of our attention.

However Thich Nhat Hahn points out that even the desire to change ourselves may be overshooting our true purpose on this planet. He writes: "You are what you want to become. Why search anymore? You are a wonderful manifestation. The whole universe has come together to make your existence possible." From this perspective we can see that even striving to transform our own inner selves is not really necessary. We already are who we long to become.

The simple message behind these teachings is to relax and recognize that you are fulfilling your purpose simply by being who you are in each and every moment, just as had been true for my father's life, which I later came to understand. Dad stopped off at the bar for a drink one night because he was just being himself and he ended up meeting a stranger who would one day bring me a message I desperately needed to hear. There is no way he could have planned that encounter or written it down as a goal for his future. Just as I could not have known that my failure to get into medical school on the first try was actually perfect and would lead me to wisdom and inspiration that I needed then and also later in my life.

Learning to be *who* we are, *wherever* we are and engaging fully in the life we have been given is what this lesson of Purpose is all about.

DETOURS ALONG THE ROAD

As we have seen before with the other lessons of this journey, there are always detours that can cause your path to swerve and branch off in a different direction than you intended. But remember that these detours actually contribute deeply to your learning experience here at Earth University—they are not negative or destructive occurrences, but part of the rich texture of life that makes every possibility available to you as an opportunity for expanding your awareness.

The first detour that is often encountered along the journey of Purpose is that of **helping.** Of course to help another and be of service can be a profound and selfless goal for life to which many of us are called. But the idea of "helping" also has a darker side. When we decide that another person "needs" our help we are marginalizing that person and viewing them as "other than" ourselves and also as "less than" ourselves. Viewing others as being in need of help implies that they are not okay just as they are, that they should change in some manner, and that we hold the answer to how they should change.

Some of us can get caught up on this detour of helping and mistake it for our life purpose. We might spend years and years in a "helping" profession with the very well-intentioned goal of making a difference in other people's lives or in our favorite cause, only to discover one day down the road that there is very little satisfaction in this type of helping. We may end up despairing over the fact that our efforts have not really made a difference at all and that the changes we were hoping to see have not happened.

I fell into this trap for a time at the shelter clinic because I was attached to the idea of "helping" the women and children there. Starting the Love Project and focusing only on loving them just as they were was the right action that brought me off the helping detour and back onto the path of Purpose.

Another detour that frequently occurs during the lesson of Purpose is that of **aspiration**, which is "the hope or ambition of achieving something." When we aspire to some goal that we want to accomplish we are projecting our energy into the future, as discussed in the previous chapter, rather than focusing it in the present moment. We commonly set goals for the future that we use for motivation, to help us focus more or work harder to get where we want to be. It's not that having a goal is a bad thing, but rather that on the detour of aspiration we tend to put all of our thoughts and energy into that goal and miss the fact that our purpose is already unfolding before our very eyes, moment to moment. Our aspirations inherently cause us to grasp and cling to future hopes and thus rob the present moment of our precious life force energy. We can spend years of our lives working toward a specific future-oriented goal before we recognize that we may never arrive at that destination.

Instead of *aspiring* toward a future goal we would be wise to become *inspired* in the present moment. With inspiration to guide us we can remain in the here and now, bring our energy and attention to whatever is unfolding in this moment, and also utilize our creativity in the current situation. When we do set goals for ourselves it is best if we focus them on the present moment: "My goal is to stay present as much as possible today, in everything I do, think and feel."

Even when we make plans for the future, which is often necessary and important, we can create those plans in the here and now, with no attachment to whether or not they actually take place. Honor the fact that there is a potential for something to occur in the future, but it may not actually happen. Then you are not clinging to the hope of a future fantasy, but instead you acknowledge that your plans are just today's idea of what may come, and everything can change in an instant.

THE EGO AND PURPOSE

> *"You wander from room to room*
> *hunting for the diamond necklace*
> *that is already around your neck."*

-RUMI

In this quote Rumi perfectly describes the dilemma of the ego as it seeks to create purpose in life. The ego searches everywhere in desperation for the sparkling jewel of Purpose that will bring value and meaning to the mundane and ordinary moments of life. This search can go on for years as the ego pursues one path after another looking for the perfect role to play. Each disappointment or downturn causes suffering as the ego copes with failure over and over again, just as I experienced when my "perfect path" to becoming a doctor, mapped out when I was 12-years-old, initially fell apart. It can take many years and many frustrations before we discover the "diamond necklace" that already hangs around our necks.

As we look more deeply it becomes apparent that Purpose has two aspects that operate simultaneously, external and internal. External Purpose has to do with the choices we make in life for our career path or occupation and how we navigate those decisions. The role of the lower self is to manage this external aspect of Purpose, by choosing a path to follow (such as becoming a doctor, in my case) and taking the necessary steps to accomplish that path (apply to medical school, attend classes, etc.) In carrying out this role the lower self might rely on previously gathered information or wisdom to chart a course for the future or might just "fly by the seat of its pants" to impulsively make choices in the moment. The lower self can receive guidance in this process from many sources, which can include the ego or Shadow or the intuitive "hits" provided by the Soul.

From the perspective of the ego, purpose involves tangible accomplishments that can be observed and measured. The ego cannot grasp the unseen or the unknowable and so purpose is viewed as a specific plan or achievement. The ego tends to choose an external path and cling to that as the reason for its existence. But there is danger within this strategy because identifying a single purpose for life can lead to despair whenever life takes an unexpected turn. The ego can be dashed over and over again in its hopes and plans to achieve a purpose as setbacks occur, as when I didn't get accepted to medical school on my first try. While it is important for the ego to identify certain milestones for purpose in life, there is also a need for flexibility and resilience in case those milestones cannot be achieved.

Ultimately, a lower self that is informed by the Soul will be able to rise above the external failures and frustrations of working toward a purpose, because the Soul provides a constant reminder of the other aspect, the Internal Purpose. The internal manifestation of purpose arises from the Galaxy view we talked about at the beginning of this book: an awareness that life is taking place on a much larger and grander scale than we can see with our eyes or know with our minds. Our own lives have a purpose that defies logic and cannot be easily charted. But from time to time we get a glimpse of this larger purpose—such as when I met the gentleman in the bar who had also met my father—and we recognize that there is no need for despair. I also had a revelation of this internal purpose for my life when at age

16 I saw that learning about *love* was the real reason for my existence.

This grand *internal* purpose always unfolds in its own time and always works out, even when we can't understand or explain why it happens that way.

The most important task for the lower self then is to chart the best course it can design, using all the knowledge, wisdom and intuitive guidance available at the time of the decision, and then let go of attachments to that purpose, which will be the focus of the next lesson. Finding purpose in life for the lower self requires constant re-evaluation and adjustments to the plan, making the best possible choices each step of the way. While the ego will still experience despair and fears of failure when plans don't work, there can be a growing awareness that somehow everything is still all right and proceeding just as it should. The ego that has learned to let go and accept things as they are will eventually find peace (the "diamond necklace" of life), no matter what path has been followed.

TRAVEL ADVISORY

Once again we look at the tricks played by the ego as it hijacks the process of spiritual growth. The ego can hide behind the façade of an apparently altruistic and "saintly" life purpose, through which it manipulates and controls other people for its own gain. While the outward appearance of this ego's purpose (such as "guru" or "spiritual leader") can suggest self-sacrifice and dedication to a higher cause, the ego is actually operating behind the scenes to seize power over others who are willing to be followers. The clever ego tricks even the "guru" into believing that he or she is fulfilling an enlightened purpose, but in fact the motivation for this "purpose" is solely for control and self-promotion. Since we live in a society where purpose is highly valued, such ego-driven leaders can quickly rise to power and fame and might lead many followers astray who long for the same popularity and control.

Within the spiritual community there have recently been many stories of such leaders from various religions whose sexual, physical or emotional abuse of students was rationalized as being necessary for the students' learning. Students and teachers alike can be confused and misled by the deceit of the ego hiding behind a spiritual disguise. Our only defense against this manipulative trick of the ego is to have a high index of suspicion as we view those with widespread influence who appear to be "too good to be true'—for there may be a power-hungry ego operating from within. We must remember that the ego favors accomplishments, possessions, control, judgments, and measurements. A leader following a true Soul Purpose will speak and relate to others with a totally different energy and affect, as we shall learn.

THE SOUL AND PURPOSE

"Sell your cleverness and buy bewilderment."

-RUMI

For the True Self or Soul, purpose is simply a state of being that arises in every moment as we live and "be" who we really are. Rumi reminds us that living our purpose doesn't require "cleverness" or a plan or scheme—even in the midst of our confusion we can still be who we are and still bring the message we came to live. It is better to set aside our intellectual seeking for purpose and just embrace the puzzling mystery of life. Then we have the greatest opportunity to "touch everything" with our pure awareness.

To understand purpose from the perspective of the True Self we need to remember that the Soul has chosen to spend a lifetime here on Earth in order to have certain experiences that are not available in the spiritual realm. The Soul attends this "Earth University" to continue it own growth and expansion. While each individual Soul has a unique curriculum during a lifetime, the overriding Soul Purpose for life is to become the best possible channel for *fearless love*. The Soul embraces suffering and difficulty in life because they are part of the process of "hollowing out" to become a better and more effective vehicle for carrying and sharing love.

Ultimately the expansion of love on this planet may require many different external paths, course corrections and "do-overs" in a single life.

The Soul accepts and even celebrates each challenge because *fearless love* becomes stronger as we move through all of life's ups and downs. There are no mistakes, no wasted moments ... not a single breath that was unnecessary or in vain.

The Soul can rejoice in the freedom and lightness of this journey that always unfolds in perfection—even though the lower self cannot perceive or imagine that perfection.

The Soul stands by as a silent witness to the glory of life, always sharing the music of the stars so that the ego can see how the dance of life has been intricately choreographed to each note. Most often the music goes unheard by the ego, too busy with planning and orchestrating to take in the melody. But when the lower self awakens, at last, to the communications of the Soul, all worry and striving can be left behind as the great cosmic dance ensues, Love shines all around, and everything changes with a single touch.

TRANSFORMING YOUR LIFE

You are facing one of the most vexing questions in human existence: What am I doing here? Asking this question is a sign that you have crossed the threshold onto the *inward arc* of your development as a spiritual being. At first you may feel lost and discouraged because this world is vast, infinitely diverse, and continually falling apart in one way or another. How can you be certain that you have any special reason for being here? That's when it becomes important to *trust* and to be *curious*.

Your life is unfolding before you one moment at a time and it is not possible to look into the future. You can see only where you have been and where you have just arrived. So moment by moment you may recognize that you are—right here, right now—where you are supposed to be, even though you don't know where you are going. Take solace in the little epiphanies, the little miracles, that you can see in this moment in time, for they are signs to reassure you that yes ... there is a reason for you to be here. Some day you will see with more clarity and understanding but for now let this moment be enough for you and look forward to whatever fascinating turns and twists life has in store on this journey from ego to Soul.

TOOLS FOR THE JOURNEY

As you seek to find your purpose in life it is most important that you remember the two aspects of purpose: internal and external. You are free to choose your external path, that is the type of work you pursue in order to support yourself and your family as you live in the world. But recognize that you also have an internal purpose that is unfolding in each moment. The more you simply focus on being your best possible self, the more you allow this internal purpose to become visible. So do your work, pursue your chosen career path, make changes whenever it feels right to you. And recognize that you will still be given opportunities to learn in life's classroom and carry on your inward journey. Check the **Resources** page for these and other tools at www.eoluniversity.com/resources

Mindset Shift

The Mindset Shift necessary to embrace your purpose is to view everything that happens as a fascinating and necessary part of your journey to becoming your best self. It is also important to remember that "you are enough" for your purpose and that you already know your next step even if you can't see it yet. In your journal write about these questions:

- How does this current situation support my internal path of growth?

- What am I learning about myself through this experience?
- How can I use this event to support my external purpose as well?
- What wisdom have I already acquired that is pointing me toward my purpose?

SHADOW WORK

Review your **Life Journey Map** and mark down the times in your life where you believe you have been a failure, where you have not succeeded at the goal or purpose you held for yourself, whether an *external* or *internal* goal. Now explore each of those events in your journal using the 3 steps of Shadow work:

1. Recognize: How have I been blaming myself for this perceived failure? How has my fear of failure interfered with my ability to make choices and take chances?

2. Recover: How can I love myself for not being perfect? How can I reframe my so-called failures and view them as learning opportunities?

3. Rise above: How can I use the wisdom I've acquired in my past failures to help me make the best choices today? How can I find gratitude for the opportunity to try again and courage to pursue new things?

Example: *One of my deepest perceived failures was not getting into medical school the first time I applied, which was an important external goal. Viewing this event as a failure caused me to doubt myself throughout my medical career and question* *whether or not I was really "good enough" to be a doctor. For my Shadow Work I needed to see why waiting a year before starting medical education was helpful for my internal growth as a person and to forgive myself (and God) for the great disappointment I felt when my plans didn't work out. Then I was able to harness gratitude for that important lesson to counter the voices in my head that told me I wasn't "good enough."*

PRACTICE

As a Practice to support your growth in purpose, focus on finding more balance in your life: between internal and external, doing and being, Heaven and Earth. The **Heaven and Earth Meditation**, which you will find fully detailed on the **Resource Page**, first leads you to imagine taking in through your feet the life-force energy from Mother Earth as a glowing liquid flame or lava. This energy supports your external purpose and your goals for your life path here on Earth. Next you visualize the life-force energy of the heavens as a ray of sunlight that enters through the top of your head. This energy supports your internal or "Soul" purpose for existence, which you want to empower in your daily life. Visualize the two energies meeting in your heart where they will work together to move you along your path and help you become your highest self. Practice this meditation once a day to help you find balance between your inner and outer aspects.

ACTION STEP

This Action Step helps you define your **Internal and External Goals** and will reinforce the idea of balancing the inner and outer forces of your life. Start with a daily planner, calendar or to-do list to record your *external goals* for each day, week, month, year, etc. Whatever system you already use to keep track of tasks you need to complete works fine for this exercise.

Next, in your journal or on a piece of paper make a list of *internal goals* that you feel would support your journey, such as starting a new daily practice, meditating more frequently, reading inspirational literature, walking in nature, listening to music, etc. Keep these goals simple and make sure you can accomplish them in 15 minutes or less. List anything that you think will help you focus *internally* on the lessons of the Soul we are studying in this book. Now return to your to-do list or calendar and add one *internal goal* for each day. You might specify a time for the goal on some days—like meditate for 15 minutes first thing in the morning. Or you can trust yourself to find time during the day between other activities.

Over time you will find it easier to incorporate *internal goals* into your life and will achieve a more natural balance between your inner and outer life. But in the beginning it helps to set aside time specifically for this important internal work.

8. THE SIXTH LESSON: SURRENDER

"Very little grows on jagged rock.
Be ground. Be crumbled,
So wildflowers will come up where you are."

-RUMI

Next we move into the sixth lesson of the inward journey, which requires us to let go of our expectations as we learn to Surrender. In the previous chapters it has already been shown that truly manifesting our Purpose in every moment calls for this very act: letting go of everything we are seeking so that we can live fully in the present moment. The lesson of Surrender requires us to go deep within as we cut away all of the attachments that would keep us stuck in the past or tied to a path of perpetual seeking. Letting go is the secret to continued growth and forward momentum as we open ourselves more and more to being perfect channels of love —to being the very ground upon which wildflowers can grow.

But life, through one difficulty after another, must turn our days of striving and grasping into the crumbled fertile soil where love eventually blossoms .

CRUMBLING GROUND

After my two-week absence, The Love Project continued to move forward, full-steam ahead, with Charlotte's re-purposed Teddy bears adding a sweet touch of comfort and healing love for our patients at the little clinic each Wednesday. The bears brought joy to both Charlotte and me because we finally had something tangible to offer that wasn't a drug or medical procedure; we could now provide our patients with a "take-home" love message.

When I marveled at Charlotte's creativity in fixing up the old bears, she revealed that she had long pursued art as a hobby. She painted on natural objects like pieces of wood or rocks that she would find while hiking in the mountains. This was an entirely new aspect of Charlotte that took me by surprise—she had hidden her creativity for the first few years of our work together because she didn't see that it had a place in the clinic.

"Work is work and fun is fun," she would say, reflecting her early years of training as a nurse. But she was beginning to understand that bringing creativity to medical care opens up possibilities for healing that science cannot explain or duplicate. She was also beginning to see the full potential of the Love Project.

One day a former resident of the shelter stopped by for a visit. She had just received her associate's degree from our local community college and wanted to show us her diploma. She also brought along a gift: she had named me the "Most Influential Person" in her life at her graduation ceremony and the college had prepared a certificate for me to hang on the wall of the clinic. I was honored and humbled to see that another person's life had been touched deeply through the Love Project at the little clinic. But to me it felt as though I had done nothing special at all—I simply showed up every Wednesday and gave my full presence and love to each person who came for an appointment. I rarely solved a medical issue, I almost never "cured" any diseases, and I didn't have any magic formula to change these troubled lives. Charlotte and I both now came to this work in service with love (and Teddy Bears) to share, but that was obviously enough. We were clearly fulfilling the purpose of the little two-room shelter clinic.

A few weeks later Charlotte arrived for our afternoon at the clinic with a gift for me: a red and tan colored quartzite stone she had polished smoothed and flat. Within the disrupted and twisting lines of color in the rock, Charlotte had visualized a scene and then outlined the picture she saw with black acrylic paint and a very fine brush. The image she had traced on the rock was a delicately drawn bear standing next to a tree trunk. I was moved by the beauty of her drawing and moreover, her creative vision to picture the bear and tree within the rock's surface. And of course … it was a bear … the perfect symbol for our work together.

Our eyes met and we both knew the significance of that gift without saying a word. We had formed a deep bond over years of working side-by-side, one that Charlotte could not express verbally but had just demonstrated to me through her thoughtful gift. I couldn't imagine a better representation of our combined effort at the clinic: as Charlotte had "released" the image of the bear from within the rock, so too had Charlotte's ability to love been released from the jagged rock of her heart.

But life was poised to ask us to let go of everything that had been accomplished at the little shelter clinic up to that point.

One Wednesday afternoon just before clinic was supposed to start I received a call from Charlotte's husband informing me that she had been rushed to a hospital in a nearby city after having a series of grand mal seizures during the night. They had discovered a brain tumor on her CT scan in the ER and she was scheduled to have surgery the next day.

After hurrying through the patients for the day, I drove straight to the hospital to see Charlotte, stopping only to buy a bouquet of wildflowers and a Teddy bear from a street vendor along the way. I didn't know if Charlotte would be conscious or able to speak but I had to see her before she underwent surgery. The procedure carried a significant risk of permanent brain damage and I desperately wanted to connect with her while I still had the opportunity. Over the years that we had worked together I had grown to love Charlotte for exactly who she was. I even loved her crusty exterior that I could finally see was just protecting the softness inside.

Charlotte was thrilled with the wildflower bouquet—as I knew she would be because of her love for the outdoors. But when I handed her the furry brown Teddy bear with a red ribbon around his neck, she burst into tears as she clutched the bear to her chest.

"You came. You came," she kept repeating through her sobs.

Once again, I didn't need to say anything—Charlotte preferred it that way. We both understood the meaning of the little bear and how much my visit meant to her at that moment. While I couldn't say in words that I cared about her, I was at least able to show her through my presence that she was important to me.

When she was able to regain her composure the first thing Charlotte said to me was "Don't give up my spot at the clinic to anyone else. I'm coming back!"

I promised her that she would always be my partner at the clinic and of course she was coming back. I would just have to make do with some substitute nurses for a few weeks while she got better. I didn't tell Charlotte but at that moment I seriously questioned whether she would ever be able to work at the clinic again.

The next day I waited by the telephone all day for word from Charlotte's husband. When he finally called the report was mixed: she had survived the surgery but because of the size of the tumor she had suffered partial paralysis on the left side of her body, which was her dominant side. At least her speech was not affected and she had a chance of regaining some function in her arm and leg with physical therapy.

Charlotte remained at a rehabilitation facility in a nearby city for the next few months and though I wasn't able to visit her there we talked briefly on the phone a few times. She reminded me during each call that she was going to come back to the clinic, and I promised, once again, that I would keep her position open.

I was still seeing patients at the little clinic each week but everything had changed. I worked with several different nurses who had volunteered to fill in and we managed to see everyone who showed up on those Wednesday afternoons but inside I felt sad and discouraged. This turn of events seemed so unfair! Charlotte had just recently been able to open her heart to our patients and find genuine joy in working there. How could it be right that all of this, along with her health and ability to function, had been taken from her so suddenly? And I felt as though the rug had been pulled out from under the Love Project—so much work over the years and just when things seemed perfect at last, it all fell apart. The Clinic of Little Miracles desperately needed a huge miracle at that moment.

Finally, after months of intense physical therapy, Charlotte was able to walk with a cane, though she still could not use her left arm or hand. She called to ask if she could be my assistant again at the clinic. Of course I said yes, though I couldn't imagine how we would make it work. I was concerned that having Charlotte trying to do intake with our patients would require some major adjustments and might be too stressful for both of us.

But when she arrived at the clinic with a huge smile on her face and a special glow about her I knew it was the right decision for her to come back. Her left arm was in a sling so she would have to do *everything, including writing, with her non-dominant right hand. This was going to be a challenge, but I was willing to give it a try.*

We organized the patients so that two of them arrived at the same time. I would take one patient into the exam room and do my own intake process and Charlotte could spend as much time as she needed with the other patient, getting her vital signs and taking notes about her condition.

On that first day it took the entire afternoon for Charlotte to prepare one patient to see me, but I didn't really mind and amazingly the patient was tolerant and understanding, as well. It was clear that Charlotte was battling major obstacles just to be there at all and the rest of us took great inspiration from her determination and perseverance. When that first patient was finally ready for me, Charlotte handed over the chart with barely legible numbers and letters on it— and somehow it was the most precious thing I had ever seen. To witness Charlotte's glowing face as she talked with each patient and to read her carefully scratched writing on the page thoroughly touched my heart. She was so dedicated and had worked so hard to be there.

After observing Charlotte in our little clinic as she coped with her physical limitations, I found that I was noticing and appreciating other people in my life who were dealing with enormous physical challenges. While I previously might not have given a thought to the man in a wheelchair in line ahead of me or make note of the struggle of a woman with a walker as she made her way down the sidewalk, I was suddenly very tuned in to those individuals. I recognized how hard they were working to carry on with the tasks of everyday life and I appreciated their determination to keep going, just as Charlotte was showing up with courage every week in our little two-room shelter clinic. I had a new perspective on suffering that I had been oblivious to before and I understood the meaning of surrender from a new point of view, as well.

Charlotte was teaching everyone at the shelter, but especially the patients and me, that you can overcome obstacles with hard work, even though you must be willing to let go of the way things were in the past. She was no longer able to rehabilitate Teddy bears for our patients so when we gave the last of the bears away we had to accept the end of that beautiful and delightful phase of our work together. She now could interact one-on-one with only two patients a day before she became exhausted.

And so each Wednesday I said a little prayer that the perfect two patients would come for Charlotte—those who would be most inspired by her presence and also be tolerant of her slowness. And I had to adjust my own expectations too. Clinic was more difficult at that point because I had less help than I had been accustomed to previously. I needed to practice patience and surrender myself as I adapted to a slower pace and less efficiency in our little clinic.

But there was something new at the clinic each Wednesday afternoon that made up for the productivity and organization we had lost. Now each time I entered the little office where Charlotte sat with a patient, I would immediately feel a sense of calmness in the room as Charlotte listened intently to every word that was being spoken. Her eyes were often filled with tears as she was moved to her core by the stories of the women and children we served. She sat quietly, listening deeply with total acceptance, in sharp contrast to those early days at the clinic when she bristled with judgment and animosity toward our patients.

Life was showing us a very different path than the one we had previously walked at the clinic, but the Love Project was still flourishing and its seeds were blossoming all around us.

In this story the lesson of Surrender came as it often does, suddenly and with great pain. Even though I had already previously surrendered to working in hospice and volunteering at the little clinic I still struggled when a new difficulty arose and I was required to surrender all the more. My ego still wanted to control the circumstances of my volunteer work and felt crushed when everything that we had worked so hard to create fell apart, not to mention the agony of seeing my friend Charlotte suffer with a life-limiting illness.

This experience provided further evidence for me that life is a continuous cycle of coming together and falling apart, which I was slowly and painfully learning. In addition, Charlotte was given the opportunity to accept her own inward journey and deal with disability and an altered lifestyle after her brain tumor. But something inspired her to want to return to the clinic and somehow I was inspired to let go of my expectations and to simply go forward with a new way of functioning.

Once again I was being shown that the "goals" I set for my lower self are often not the same as the lessons that my Soul is learning on the Galaxy level of life. After Charlotte's surgery and recovery it became clear that our work at the clinic was as much about each one of us and our own personal growth as it was about the growth and healing of our patients.

That's the beauty of this inward journey: when you recognize that your own falling apart and gradual recovery provides exactly the "crumbled ground" within which another person can bloom.

THE PATH OF SURRENDER

When we reach the lesson of Surrender we have arrived at a place on our inward journey that very few people within

Western society ever visit. The idea of surrendering, which is often equated with "giving up," runs counter to the fierce determination and courageous perseverance that we value and admire. The concept of Surrender is often misunderstood within our culture and particularly the medical system. Doctors vow that they will not surrender against diseases like cancer as they continue to recommend treatments with very little chance of benefit. Patients are encouraged to "keep fighting" in the battle that is being waged and are praised for refusing to give up. Families agree with medical providers to keep loved ones alive using artificial means, often inflicting suffering, because they feel it would be unloving to "give up hope" and stop waiting for a miracle to occur.

But in each of these circumstances there is a detrimental misinterpretation of the lesson of Surrender. To surrender to illness and eventually death, from a spiritual perspective, is to embrace the idea that life and death occur within their own time frames and truly are not under our control. To surrender is to allow the natural process to take place, while working to find the deepest meaning and the most growth possible within the current circumstances. This is not to say that extreme medical treatment is always unwarranted, because there are definitely situations in which lives are saved that would have been lost without intervention. We need discernment to know when it is appropriate to act and when it is wise to let go. Too often in our medical system the default choice is to "do everything possible" even though there is evidence that some patients live longer and with greater quality of life when aggressive treatment is stopped and hospice care is offered instead.

Charlotte's determination to return to the clinic demonstrates the delicate balance that is required when we learn to surrender to whatever life is bringing us. She didn't linger in anger or bitterness over the difficulty that had befallen her and she didn't give up in despair and apathy. She chose to work hard within the limitations of her condition to be the best self she could be. She simultaneously accepted the reality of the change that had occurred in her health, let go of her expectations for the future, and worked to create a "new normal" in her life. The key to Charlotte's ability to find this balance was the fact that she had embraced a higher purpose for her existence. Her work at the clinic provided her with meaning and fulfillment and she chose to focus on this path of giving to others from whatever measure of abundance she possessed, even while coping with the aftermath of a brain tumor. From this Galaxy-level perspective, Charlotte recognized that she could fulfill her purpose of caring for others no matter what difficulties arose in her life.

In 7 *Lessons for Living from the Dying* we learned the story of Ashley, a young woman with a neuromuscular disorder who had been bedridden and intellectually challenged since early childhood. But for all of her physical and mental difficulties, Ashley could still smile and bless the lives of everyone in her presence by speaking the only three words she knew: "I love you." She had no choice but to surrender to her illness, just as Charlotte could not control the fact that she had developed a life-threatening brain tumor. But Ashley still managed to bring love to the planet in her own way, as did Charlotte when she returned to our little clinic.

From a spiritual perspective *fighting against* an illness or injury or any other difficulty of life means resisting the process that is naturally occurring and expending energy to try to force a different outcome. In the end this resistance is futile and actually drains the energy of everyone involved while diverting focus in the wrong direction. The lesson of Surrender teaches that it is important to accept the current situation and *work within it* to create new possibilities and a new reality. The emphasis of the medical system on curing and eliminating disease tends to ignore the fact that true healing lies within each person rather than in some external treatment. As a reflection of this desire to find "cures" for every type of suffering in existence, our society overvalues the idea of "health" and despises illness, infirmity, frailty and pain.

Yet, as we have already seen, suffering is the threshold of the inward journey—the point at which transformation and growth become possible. To find the True Self we must learn to utilize everything that life offers to us on our journey. We must find ways to dig deep into our Shadow and heal the old wounds that cause us to fear and resist the natural falling apart that happens in every lifetime. Then we will be able to navigate our difficulties with grace and curiosity while we simply show up each day and live the best life possible within our circumstances.

However even in spiritual circles the lesson of Surrender is sometimes misinterpreted. In many groups the act of surrender is defined as giving up one's personal will to follow a teacher or guru. The follower renounces his or her own guidance and turns over everything to the teacher. This type of surrender shows devotion and selflessness but may be misguided. For in reality we are each meant to fully become our own unique selves here on this planet. Blindly following the direction of any other person, no matter how wise, does not actually help us grow in consciousness, but can lead to confusion and repression of our own individuality.

The Universe doesn't produce clones; it seeks maximum diversity in creation, as evidenced by the profusion of various plant and animal species in nature. To surrender is actually to allow this diversity to unfold in its splendor in our own lives, unhindered by our attempts to control the outcome of every event. The act of surrender also requires us to accept that falling apart is the process by which growth occurs. We will have to fall apart over and over again, as I was learning in the little clinic, in order to grow into our True Selves and become the best possible people we can be.

So you can surrender to the inevitable course of an illness, as Charlotte did, but use the illness itself as a motivator for growth and change. Rather than resist the challenges brought about by illness, find a way to work within them and still become the best person you can be. If continued treatment is futile or even harmful, stop it and focus instead on the quality of each day. If a loved one is being kept alive physically solely through mechanical means, consider surrendering to the illness or injury that has taken away the life force and allowing the body to experience its natural death. If you wish to pursue a spiritual path, find a teacher that honors your uniqueness and doesn't require you to give up your identity. Instead go within and discover the growth that awaits you there—you already know everything you need to know. Your spiritual path requires you to surrender the idea that you must search outside of yourself for answers and wake up instead to the fact that you already possess the answers within you. But you won't be able to see those answers until further along your journey, when the timing is right.

THE WISDOM OF SURRENDER

"Completion comes not from adding another piece to ourselves, but from surrendering our ideas of perfection."

- MARK EPSTEIN

Ultimately the process of Surrender has to do with letting go of our ideas of how things *should be* and our attachments to an expectation for the future. To surrender is to live with equanimity in a state of "not-knowingness," admitting that we don't have the answers for life and we don't even have the best vision for how the future should unfold. This sort of surrender allows us to live life peacefully but with a constant sense of curiosity about why things happen the way they do and what might be coming next. Once you let go of the false notion that you can and should control everything in your life you will begin to live with a sense of freedom and completion as in the quote above by Mark Epstein.

Lao-Tzu, a Chinese philosopher from the 5th century BCE and the author of the *Tao Te Ching,* wrote; "When I let go of what I am, I become what I might be." The best way to manifest your full potential in this life is to surrender your attachments to who you think you are or how your life is supposed to be. While you make decisions for your life such as choosing your career path and relationships, you should not be attached to any particular outcome. You do not know where anything will lead or what disruptions will happen, including illness, injury, loss, and also joyful surprises and miracles.

The only thing you know for certain is that you will receive opportunities on this life-path of yours to learn what you need to learn.

You may think you are on one particular path, headed in a certain direction, with many likely or predictable outcomes. But any type of disruption to your journey can occur at any time. Be prepared for and curious about anything that may come your way—life gets really interesting when you hold it lightly and see it from the Galaxy view.

Rumi wrote: "Keep walking though there's no place to get to. Don't try to see through the distances--that's not for human beings. Move within, but don't move the way fear makes you move." He reminds us that the act of surrendering is not just a passive process of giving up. To truly surrender requires us to make choices and keep moving through our lives rather than to just allow events to happen to us.

So chart the best course for your life and then watch to see what unfolds. Be ready at any time to switch tracks, to readjust and to expand your view. Continue to accept whatever comes and understand that you can't see everything, even from the Galaxy view. Your vision is still limited and you don't know the whole story right now. So choose the best option available to you —the one that includes the most love and feels the most relaxed to you in the moment. Also remember that whatever you don't learn now you can still learn later—life will keep offering you chances to discover everything you need to know.

DETOURS ALONG THE ROAD

As we have seen before on this inward journey there are many detours that can turn our direct route to enlightenment into a winding, circuitous trail. We can become "stuck" for a time in any number of bypasses as we work through complex Shadow issues or gather more nuanced information about the lesson we are working on. But these deviations from the path are never a mistake and usually hold crucial learning opportunities for us, no matter how long they seem to detain our growth.

One of the common detours on the journey of Surrender is **intellectualism** or a belief that through knowledge one can gain ultimate control over life and its circumstances. With an emphasis on the importance of education, our Western society encourages and supports the attainment of knowledge throughout life, which in itself is quite a good thing. But the very act of filling the mind with information seems to convey to some a false sense of power or control over life and the world. Time is spent pondering and arguing about the situations that life creates; energy is expended on technology and developments that have the intention of providing greater control over life; and those with less education are pitied for their ignorance. Some of us seek out more and more education, acquiring numerous degrees and titles along the way.

But this intellectual gluttony fosters an arrogance toward life that is soon shattered by the onset of difficulties that cannot be controlled or explained. Many of us have experienced an intellectual phase on our journeys when we too believed that because of our superior knowledge, destiny was in our own hands and we could create the life of our dreams. This phase is often toppled when the uncertainties of existence rise up and prove that control is an illusion. Then some journeyers become totally disheartened and bitter when their rational constructs fail them during a time of crisis and can sink into depression and despair. Without sufficient tools to help them cope with difficulty they might enter another detour of grief that can last for many years. The ultimate message is to pursue as much education as you desire, but don't fail to do your own inner work during your schooling. In fact, dedicate your institutional education in service of your spiritual education and you will find many opportunities to deepen your heart's wisdom while you stretch your intellect.

Another tricky detour on the road of spiritual growth is **hypervigilance**, which can lead some to take too much responsibility for the outcome of life's challenges. People who get trapped on this bypass often have a great deal of compassion and feel it is their duty or mission to protect others from harm. They may take on the problems and pain of other people and work tirelessly to try to fix what is going wrong in their lives. But they have not yet understood that each person is on their own unique journey and will experience the lessons needed during this lifetime. A hypervigilant person loses focus on her own journey while tending to everyone else's pain and thus forgets to do her own inner work.

This was part of the problem I was having when I first started seeing patients at the shelter clinic. I took it upon myself to try to resolve the suffering of each person until I recognized (with the help of the homeless man, Ben) that I was not responsible for anyone else and kindness was all that was needed. Once I began the Love Project I was able to find my way back to the path and begin anew the process of learning the lessons the clinic could teach me. And ironically it was only when I stopped trying to help the shelter residents fix their lives that the Love Project actually began to make a difference for some of them.

The third detour that can occur during the lesson of Surrender is simply **guilt**. It is difficult to let go of our expectations and feelings of responsibility for others without wondering if we are shirking our duty or being selfish. In fact when we stop trying to control everything around us it may seem as if others will suffer without our advice and guidance. Guilt can cause us to stay in unhealthy circumstances that do not support growth because we fear letting another person down or not fulfilling our responsibilities. But those fears arise from a misunderstanding of surrender: when we let go of control we actually become more helpful to others and more capable of responding to difficulties.

With our energy in the present moment, unattached to any

expectations, we can sense more accurately how to connect with anyone and what action is needed from us in any situation. Surrender is ultimately the path to becoming a true blessing to others and to the world as we travel unencumbered by limiting beliefs and demands. Charlotte had no choice but to surrender to her partial paralysis after her brain surgery. But through her acceptance of her limitations she became a more powerful channel for *fearless love* to our patients.

THE EGO AND SURRENDER

*"Don't push the river,
It flows by itself"*

-ROBIN CAASDAN

This piece of advice from Robin Caasdan represents the precise message that the lower self struggles to grasp on its journey to awakening. The ego has the mistaken notion that it can control the events and outcomes of life, and this belief is often reinforced by society and even by pseudo-spiritual teachings. The idea that one can create reality and manifest desires is very seductive to the lower self and ego, leading to a false sense of control over life itself. But the ego is oblivious to the flow of the Universe and does not recognize that life has its own timing and agenda. Likewise, the ego is unaware of the Soul lessons that are part of this life journey and has no idea that no matter how hard it tries to push, life will flow in its own direction.

The act of surrender makes no sense to the lower self, especially to the ego, because it is equated with admitting defeat and handing over control to someone or something more powerful. This conflicts with the ego's primary concern for survival and seems to represent a serious threat to existence so the ego will always resist surrendering. However the ego misunderstands the higher definition of surrender and fails to see that rather than leading to a loss of freedom, the act of surrendering actually creates even more freedom and expansiveness. Letting go of futile attempts to control what cannot be controlled frees up energy for creativity and growth. Lao-Tzu wrote, "To hold, you must first open your hand. Let go." So letting go is actually the paradoxical secret to having what is needed. Going with the flow of life is actually much more productive than trying to "push the river."

Ultimately the lower self is asked to surrender to the guidance of the Soul but this cannot occur until the lower self awakens and the ego's fear of annihilation is overcome.

The ego must recognize that its purpose is to be a vehicle for the Soul, like the tiger trained by the goddess Durga, assisting the Soul's journey on this planet and manifesting the gifts of the Soul into physical reality. Everything the ego longs for is available through its integration with the Soul but that requires surrender, which the mind and the ego have long been conditioned to resist.

The ego, lacking wholeness, operates through greed and fear: hoarding its possessions and defending itself against higher wisdom. But ironically the very surrender the ego fears most is the one act that will provide ultimate fulfillment and peace.

TRAVEL ADVISORY

As with previous lessons, there is also a possibility that the newly awakened ego can hijack the process of spiritual growth and exhibit a false substitute for the true act of Surrender. In this case the ego gives lip service to the idea of surrender and may talk and teach about the concept. But in reality that ego remains attached to expectations and desires and operates behind the scenes as a means of gaining more control. We might believe that we have fully let go of our need to be in control as long as there is no challenge to our power. But certain situations where we cannot secretly manipulate others may reveal to us that the ego is still holding on to control and trying to "push the river."

Sometimes the ego reveals itself through the nature of spiritual practice itself. A controlling ego might use prayer to ask for specific outcomes and "suggest" to God what should happen next. But a true act of surrender leads to prayer simply for the highest good of all, without a self-motivated agenda or a list of requests. In fact, true surrender doesn't demand rigidity or strict rules for spiritual behavior at all. When expectations are released then everything can flow naturally, including prayer and spiritual devotion. There is no longer any need for guidelines and regulations. A sure sign of disguised ego is a reliance on spiritual rules to govern the behavior of self and others. The act of surrender fosters listening quietly for guidance whispered softly from the Soul.

THE SOUL AND SURRENDER

"This universe is not outside of you.
Look inside yourself;
everything that you want, you are already that."

-RUMI

From the perspective of the Soul, there is no need to surrender for already the Soul does not cling or grasp for anything. The Soul flourishes in the emptiness of each and every moment and yet lacks for nothing. The Soul looks upon the struggles of the lower self and ego with compassion, gently encouraging the letting-go of attachments, the realization that everything the lower self desires already exists within.

Nothing is viewed as good or bad to the Soul, nothing is a mistake. Life flows with its own timing and everything is accepted.

Because the past and future do not exist, the Soul sees only the perfection of this moment and would change nothing about the here and now but lets it all go in the next moment and the next.

The Soul recognizes that when the lower self and ego finally learn to surrender, then the wildflowers of purpose can bloom and manifest their highest potential; then unconditional love can flourish and no resentments will be held; then suffering will be perceived as simply the process necessary to become crumbled ground. Letting go of every expectation and every desire is the path toward ultimate fulfillment and meaning in life.

TRANSFORMING YOUR LIFE

This lesson of Surrender is one of the trickiest stages of your spiritual development, but one of the most important. As a human being you are hard-wired to resist what appears negative or "bad" and to seek out pleasure, certainty and comfort instead. Yet in this lesson you are being asked to let go of your resistance to the falling apart of your life and simply "go with the flow" of your current circumstances. Nothing about this makes sense or seems advisable to your lower self.

Surrender requires intentional choice and effort to rise above the warnings of your ego/mind and the desire to fight against what is viewed as wrong. But surrender does not mean giving up or becoming apathetic to what is out of alignment in our society. When you surrender you acknowledge that much of life is out of your control and you do not know the outcome of your work. But you carry on with your work nonetheless.

You can continue being an activist for the good—for Love over Fear—but you must become a *contemplative activist*. In this role you will measure every word and step carefully and not be controlled by anger but harness it to take powerful actions on behalf of the good of all, like the goddess Durga. A practice of deep contemplation will lead you to the wisdom you need to make the best choices and use your life-force energy strategically to help the world change and grow.

TOOLS FOR THE JOURNEY

The central task for the lesson of Surrender is learning to let go of control. Because the ego has a strong primal need to be in charge in order to provide protection from danger we face a daily struggle to remember that we really do not control most of the circumstances of our lives. Giving up control and the belief that we always know what is right can have powerful benefits as we relax into the ease of allowing things to be as they are and going with the flow of life. Check the **Resources** page for these and other tools at www.eoluniversity.com/resources

MINDSET SHIFT

An important Mindset Shift to help you learn to surrender is to understand that pain is better managed when we allow it to be part of our lives rather than trying to resist or destroy it. This includes pain we are experiencing now and pain from the past. In your journal write about your current pain, whether emotional or physical:

- How am I resisting discomfort right now?
- How can I allow it to simply be there for as long as it needs to be?
- What am I trying to control in my life right now?
- What have I invested my energy and expectation in for the future?

SHADOW WORK

On your **Life Journey Map** make note of any times when you tried desperately to control a situation you were in or another person, in order to force a certain outcome that you wanted. Now explore each of those events in your journal using the 3 steps of Shadow work:

1. Recognize: When do I feel frustrated because I cannot control what is happening around me? When do I resist changes because they don't meet my expectations? How attached am I to my hopes for the future?

2. Recover: When has change actually led to something good in my life that I wasn't expecting? How can I find hope instead of fear about the future?

3. Rise above: What will it take to help me feel safe enough to stop trying to control situations that are out of my control? How can I get comfortable not knowing what the future holds for me?

Example: *When my book **What Really Matters** was first published I created a long list of tasks for myself to market and promote the book. I believed I should be in total control of how the book got out to the world. But a few days after the release I was in a biking accident and suffered a concussion and broken collarbone. All of my planning had been for nothing as I had to spend a few quiet months recovering from the concussion. During that time I had plenty of opportunity to reflect and learn to let go of my need to control. I discovered that there are times when spontaneity is much more productive than over-planning.*

PRACTICE

The **Bridge Meditation** is a practice to remind you to let go of your efforts to control things and accept the flow of life. You'll find more details about it on the **Resource Page**. If you

live near water, such as a stream or river, you can do this practice in nature to help you experience the energy of flowing
water. But you can also just visualize this entire exercise with
your eyes closed. Stand on a bridge that crosses the water and
face downstream, so you can see the water flow away from you.
Take a few deep breaths and imagine releasing all of the things
you can no longer control or that no longer serve you into the
water. Watch them flow away from you until you feel lighter
inside. Then turn to the other side of the bridge and face
upstream. Imagine that the water flowing toward you is washing
you clean and bringing you new and unexpected blessings to
replace what you have released.

The **Serenity Practice** can also help you begin to let go
of some of your attempts to control your life. You'll find a
complete description and worksheet on the **Resource Page**.
Begin by making a list of everything in your daily that currently
upsets you. What issues come to mind that frequently cause you
to feel annoyed? Make a vertical list of these items.

Next review each item and decide whether or not it is something that you could realistically change if you tried (e.g. Your
haircut, your messy work environment, a co-worker who
constantly interrupts you, etc.) Write CAN next to each item
that you believe you can change.

Write CANNOT next to any items that you could never
change (e.g. your eye color, the weather, rush hour traffic, etc.)

Now review the items marked CAN and circle any of them
that you seriously WANT to change and would be willing to
invest time and energy to change. Make a list of these circled
items and use it as a reminder to work toward productive change
in your life as you move forward.

With the remaining items on the list that you either
CANNOT change or don't care enough to change, visualize
stepping away from them and withdrawing your energy from

them. Focus on making peace with these issues and gradually letting go of each one.

Action Step

A simple Action Step to reinforce what you are learning about Surrender is to **Give Away** or let go of one item in your life that you no longer need. It might be a material possession or a relationship or an attitude or a habit. Whatever you choose, take a committed step toward releasing it from your life: give something to a Thrift Store, write a letter to someone, get a new haircut, throw away an unhealthy snack from your cabinet. You will be proving to yourself that it is relatively easy to let go of things that don't serve you which is the first task of Surrender. Then you will create more space and energy to allow you to accept all the aspects of life that you cannot control or change.

9. THE SEVENTH LESSON: IMPERMANENCE

"Regard this fleeting world
as a star at dawn, a bubble in a stream,
a flash of lightning in a summer cloud
a flickering lamp — a phantom — and a dream."

-BUDDHA

The final stop on our inward journey of spiritual transformation bring us to the lesson of Impermanence. Our ultimate task is to remember that we are spiritual beings who reside in physical bodies that will one day fall away. We are asked to revel in this physical existence while we have it and to experience each moment to the fullest whether it brings us joy or pain. And simultaneously we must hold the knowledge that every blessing, every sorrow, every miracle and every difficulty will soon fade away like a dream. Everything will ultimately fall apart but whatever exists in this moment is meant to be cherished and celebrated right here, right now. This is the ultimate lesson we grapple with when we take our final breaths in human form and gradually dissolve back into the light from which we came.

A FLASH OF LIGHTNING

Over the next few months Charlotte and I settled into a "new normal" in our little shelter clinic as she dealt with the aftermath of her brain surgery. We continued to receive exactly what was needed for each patient, but now I noticed tears in Charlotte's eyes every time a new "little miracle" appeared. She never talked about her own health status so I didn't know what her prognosis was or what to expect in the future, but that's how Charlotte wanted it—privacy was very important to her. So we both just showed up on Wednesday after-noons and I felt grateful each week that Charlotte was still able to come to our special little clinic. However, knowing the seriousness of her medical condition, I was prepared that things could change at any time—I just didn't realize how that change might materialize.

Later that summer something totally unexpected occurred when my husband received an offer for his "dream job" in another state. He had waited a long time for such an opportunity to arise so with little hesitation we made a family decision to move from our comfortable home and begin a new journey. As life would have it, we had to pack up and leave within two weeks so that our children could start the school year on time in our new location. Like a flash of lightning, everything changed in an instant. There was no time to gradually withdraw from the work I was doing, to say an adequate goodbye to every person I cared about, or to tie up all the loose ends that had been left dangling through the years. Life was asking me to change and to do it rapidly.

Though I was excited for the opportunity to live in a new place, I agonized over leaving behind the work that I loved. I was still employed by a local hospice and also served as the medical director for a nursing home, along with my volunteer work at the shelter clinic. Each of these jobs was special to me and had taught me so much about life and death and spiritual growth. My heart was breaking at the thought of leaving behind the patients and staff members I had come to love and especially at the prospect of saying goodbye to Charlotte. I had prepared myself for the possibility of Charlotte's death but had not considered that I might be the one to leave behind the little clinic and our special Love Project.

However before I could even begin to stress over who would fill the positions I was vacating, life provided another little miracle for me. Just as we finalized our decision to move I had an unexpected phone call from an old friend from residency training who had just left his medical practice. He told me he was searching for more mean-ingful work—just like I had found in hospice and at the shelter clinic. Miraculously my sudden move provided just the opportunity he needed to find meaning in medicine once again. He stepped up and took over my two medical director jobs and the volunteer work at the shelter clinic, happy to have a chance to give back to others, while I was relieved to have found my own replacement for the work I cared about so much. In the midst of my hectic packing and cleaning I marveled at how perfectly I was being assisted during this process of sudden change. I could only hope that my parting with Charlotte would work out equally well.

I planned to tell Charlotte about our upcoming move at the end of the day on my second-to-last Wednesday in the little clinic so that she would have a week to adjust before our final farewell. She was clearly shocked when she heard my news but, true to her old form, didn't say a word to me as she gathered her things and left for the day. I was hopeful that we could say a proper goodbye the next week after she had a little time to adjust to this sudden change.

But when I arrived for that final day at the clinic I found that there were no appointments scheduled because the shelter staff and residents had planned a going-away party for me. It was a wonderful surprise and gave me a chance to say goodbye to everyone I had come to know over the past seven years. They had prepared a luncheon for me, with a special cake and a bouquet of flowers, which was delightful ... but someone was missing.

Throughout the festivities I kept looking around the room for Charlotte and couldn't find her anywhere. I had brought a farewell gift for her that I knew she would love: a small feather delicately carved from wood and painted the colors of a mountain bluebird's wing. At the end of the day I still had not seen Charlotte anywhere and was worried that she might be sick. But a friend of hers who also volunteered at the shelter told me that Charlotte didn't come that day because "she doesn't do goodbyes."

I couldn't bear the thought of moving away without a chance to see Charlotte one more time, so after the party I drove to her house to look for her. When I arrived her car was in the driveway and I assumed that she was home, but no one answered my knock on the door. Not knowing what else to do I sat down on the front steps and waited to see if she would eventually appear. As the minutes ticked by I realized that I might never see her again and tears began to roll softly down my cheeks. My heart broke open in that moment.

There was so much I needed to say to Charlotte—to tell her what our journey together at the clinic had meant to me and that I loved her. We had been through so much together. She had helped me learn to love the unlovable parts of her and of myself as well, and now I could finally see the beauty that lies within everyone. I wanted to give her my gift of the painted feather so that she would have it to remember me by just as I had the rock she painted for me as a keepsake.

After waiting a full hour I reluctantly had to leave to finish packing before the movers arrived the next morning. I hastily scrawled a goodbye note to her and left it on the porch along with the little box *that held the wooden feather. Then I walked away with the sad knowledge that I would most likely never see Charlotte's face again.*

The next few months were hectic with unpacking, settling into a new house, getting familiar with a new community, and starting a new job. I was deeply disappointed over the fact that there was no hospice work for me there so I had to accept a position once more in a family medicine clinic. I couldn't at all understand this turn of events: I had finally found the perfect work for me in hospice where I had been able to heal my grief, discover what really matters in life, and find meaning in medical practice again. When that work came to an end with our move I was crushed, but I had to surrender to the change. Once again life was teaching me that nothing lasts, everything changes, and each day is a new opportunity for growth.

However shortly after our move I learned that there was a tiny volunteer clinic in my new community that offered care to low-income individuals and happened to be in desperate need of a medical director. So just like that I was already being shown the next step on my inward journey. Even though it hurt to lose my work in hospice I could see that I was still being watched over and provided with exactly what I needed on this spiritual path. It turned out that my work at the little shelter clinic had perfectly prepared me for this new project. So I simply had to humble myself, let go of my attachments to how things used to be and move forward with curiosity into another "new normal" just as I had learned to do over and over again throughout the past.

Things keep falling apart so that we can dig deep, expose what has been hidden and find our True Selves—that's what makes growth possible. As time went on in my new life I was gradually able to adapt to all of the changes that had taken place so quickly, like a flash of lightning, without warning.

Several months later I received a phone call from Charlotte's husband letting me know that she had died. Her brain tumor had returned shortly after I moved away and had grown so rapidly that no treatment had been possible. He told me he believed that Charlotte might have died after her first surgery if she hadn't been so deter-mined to come back to the little shelter clinic. Working there had given her a reason to go on living against all odds. He thanked me profusely for welcoming Charlotte back to the clinic after her surgery and said that it meant everything to her.

I was grateful to him for calling—and though I still wished I could have seen Charlotte one last time, at least I was able to find some closure by telling her husband how much I loved her.

"She knew that," he reassured me, to my surprise.

But then I remembered that all along Charlotte and I had been able to communicate with very few words. We had understood one another without talking about it—and in a way it all seemed perfect. Charlotte was gone, the Love Project was finished, the little miracles had ceased, and it was time for that part of the story to come to an end. But over the years to follow I would look back with reverence on those days of simplicity, surprises, Teddy bears, and making the best of whatever life had to offer in the little two-room shelter clinic on Wednesday afternoons.

In this final story I had to struggle with the fact that nothing lasts and everything changes. Even those things that are beautiful and meaningful must ultimately fall away when their time comes to an end. I was confused by the fact that our family's move required me to leave my work in hospice and that I wasn't able to say goodbye to Charlotte before her death. I wondered why life had unfolded that way but that question has remained unanswered, just as many of life's mysteries are never resolved. Change arrived for me and for Charlotte without any warning and once again there was no choice but to accept it and move on. My lower self struggled to surrender to change even though

I was provided with all of the support and opportunity I needed in order to move forward in a new setting. In looking back at the story of the little clinic I could see perfection in each experience as Charlotte and I were being shaped and transformed by the Love Project. But it was not meant to last forever. I was learning this gritty lesson of impermanence in the only way it can be taught—by experiencing one change after another.

THE PATH OF IMPERMANENCE

The opportunity to master this final lesson of Impermanence often comes with significant pain, as it did for me and for Charlotte when I had to leave the little clinic we had created together. Impermanence requires the ultimate letting go of everything that has been cherished in life, including relationships, meaningful work, and even physical existence itself. As human beings we naturally cling to whatever brings us joy and also to those things that seem important to our survival. There is no easy way to let go of these deep attachments of our lives, but the spiritual journey gives us no other choice. Everything that we have valued eventually leaves us and we cannot stop the process. The poet Rainer Maria Rilke wrote: "Life blows away, always." So we are left stunned by the side of the road as we watch everything we have known dissolve into dust and be carried from our hands on the passing breeze. This is the daunting nature of the lesson of Impermanence that we are asked to master.

The impetus to move to a new community came like a flash of lightning for my family and me, unexpected and brilliant in its own way. Clearly this change was the right thing, there was no arguing that, but the cost of the transition was dear. I struggled to maintain my equanimity during the process because I still longed to control the events of life and believed that I could foresee the perfect outcome. Leaving my work with hospice and the little clinic was nearly overwhelming for me. But it was saying goodbye to Charlotte, knowing I would never see her again, that was particularly painful. I clung to the idea of a heartfelt farewell that would provide me the opportunity to say to her all the things that had never been spoken before—and I had imagined a final conversation with her that would provide both of us with closure. But that was not what happened and my ultimate heartache came from the shattering of that dream. Once again there was no choice. I had to let go. I had to move on. My hospice work, the clinic, the Love Project, and Charlotte all were blowing away from me in that moment.

In this human existence we are constantly asked to accept change as we grow and mature. Even from one day to the next nothing really stays the same. But we have a necessary illusion of constancy that helps us feel safe and grounded. When we have lived in the same place for some time we stop noticing the natural changes that take place in our surroundings. We don't recognize the fading paint on the walls, the wearing down of the floorboards, the trees in the yard growing taller, or the shingle that has come loose on the roof unless something wakes us up and causes us to pay attention. With repetition and sameness comes a certain blindness, as our brains take a shortcut and show us familiar images from the past as a background rather than a detailed picture of the current situation. So we forget that everything is constantly changing and constantly falling apart. We become complacent and comfortable with the idea that we can expect things to be pretty much the same tomorrow and the next day as they were yesterday and today.

But the flash of lightning and the ripple in the stream come to wake us up, to help us see through our illusion that everything will remain the same.

In that moment of awakening we stand breathless as our attachments are painfully ripped away and we learn all over again that nothing lasts. In that instant, as we see everything dissolve and blow away, we may not remember that this change is precisely the process that will allow something new to arise, that will allow life to continue, that actually spawns hope for the future. For just that one moment we find that we too are dissolving away, we see that even our own existence is an illusion, we recognize that everything is part of something much greater, and everything is perfect.

This awareness is the hidden gem that lies within all suffering and loss. But it arises briefly, like the star at dawn, and then is quickly eclipsed by the emotion that swells inside of us. Pain overtakes us in the next moment and we fall to our knees with the sorrow of this human life. This lesson of Impermanence is learned gradually and slowly over time, through one loss after another. Nothing can stop the changes that come to us and nothing can stop the pain we feel except continuing to grow in our awareness and our ability to let go.

THE WISDOM OF IMPERMANENCE

"Remember always that you are just a visitor here, a
*   traveler passing through.*
Your stay is but short and the moment of your departure

unknown."

-BHANTE DHAMMIKA

Ultimately the lesson of Impermanence is meant to teach us exactly what this passage says: our stay here is short and we have no idea when it will come to an end. This message is echoed in the writings of all wisdom traditions throughout time. Yet it is one of the most challenging concepts we struggle to grasp and live by. We see ourselves as the superior creation on this planet, with physical prowess over many of our fellow creatures and consciousness that surpasses all other life forms. It seems only natural that our survival as a species is of utmost importance here and that our individual lives are equally valuable. However transcending this limited awareness is necessary for our spiritual growth and all great spiritual teachers have spoken of this vital and painful awareness that eludes us for most of our lives.

But why is this knowledge so important for us to recognize? The 5th century BCE Chinese philosopher Lao Tzu wrote: "If you realize that all things change, there is nothing you will try to hold on to." Since our natural tendency is to resist change and hold on to the past, we can occupy ourselves for most of our years with futile attempts to keep life "the same as it always has been." We frequently hear calls from politicians and would-be leaders to return to the "good old days" when life was easier, they say, and somehow all positive. Of course those memories of good days in the past are just idealized illusions that we cling to in our minds because they provide us with security and solace. But there is no returning to what was—that cannot happen.

The Greek philosopher Heraclitus wisely wrote: "No man

ever steps in the same river twice, for it's not the same river and he's not the same man." All of life flows like the river and blows like the wind. There is no repeating of the past or even containing a single moment to keep it from changing. Yet we spend countless hours of our lives trying to do exactly that and we have a marketing and advertising system in place that encourages this very futile journey. By filling our sight and minds with visions of "eternal youth," unlimited virulence, prevention of aging, and perpetual health, we are fed fantasies of a life that is within our control, that can serve our every whim and play out exactly as we script it, if only we purchase the right products or follow the right teachers.

But again that is all an illusion—lies we tell ourselves rather than face the truth of this earthly existence. This is how it really goes: we are enrolled in a school of suffering and we have many lessons to learn. Life will continually provide us with opportunities to learn these lessons and we have the freedom to refuse them to a certain point. We aren't required to learn anything, but much of our misery will come from this refusal.

In fact, Thich Nhat Hahn, Vietnamese monk and Zen master, has written, "Once we recognize that all things are impermanent, we have no problem enjoying them." So our erroneous belief is that we must control everything and keep it from changing or we will fall apart. But in reality, we can only know true joy if we embrace the idea of impermanence and let go of all our manipulations and calculations. This is the supreme paradox of life itself! We can only enjoy what we are willing to release; trying to "squeeze" the pleasure out of life by holding onto it is exactly what destroys our ability to be fully alive and enjoy every moment.

Furthermore, Lao Tzu also wrote, "If you are not afraid of dying, there is nothing you cannot achieve." So our ability to fulfill our purpose and make a difference in the world also depends upon our willingness to accept impermanence. Losing our fear of dying is the greatest task in this lesson of Impermanence and is hard to accomplish without some extraordinary life event. Those who have faced life-limiting illness or had a near-death experience often report that their fear has vanished after brushing up against death in an undeniable fashion. Hospice workers and caregivers who spend time at the bedside of dying patients also express a diminished fear of death and an ever-present awareness of the fleeting nature of life, like "a flash of lightning in a summer cloud."

This is the ultimate goal for each of us: to confront our deep-seated fear of death and choose to live life fully with the knowledge that all of this will be gone in an instant, at any time.

That is a huge task for each of us to take on but our own lives and the survival of our planet depend upon it. Our spiritual growth and expansion of consciousness cannot occur without this crucial awakening.

DETOURS ALONG THE ROAD

As with each of the lessons along this inward journey, we are likely to spend some time on significant "alternate paths" as we make our way to greater awareness. Each of these detours can occupy our time for a great many years, yet if they are part of the journey, then they are perfect in their own way. Every learning experience is important for our ultimate awakening so we can embrace our journey exactly as it has unfolded with total acceptance.

One of the most common detours that can distract us from the lesson of Impermanence is **belief**, which means placing our trust or confidence in something outside of ourselves. At certain stages along the inward journey we might look for reassurance and safety from institutions or systems that help us cope with being human. Affiliating with a concern that is larger and more stable than our own reality can assist us as we negotiate the difficulties of life and can give us hope for the future. But our beliefs can also lead to denial of our own impermanence. We can believe in a religion and cling to the idea that our faith will protect us from unwanted change and the specter of death.

Likewise many of us believe in science, medicine and technology and trust that somehow there will be antidotes for everything we fear, including our own mortality. We can also believe in various causes, political groups, social organizations, alternative therapies, exercise modalities, hobbies, and even money as the answer to the impermanence that we dread. The problem with relying on such belief systems is that the focus is on wisdom from a source outside of ourselves, which prevents us from hearing our own internal guidance. The belief that any external system has answers for us is another illusion that we cling to in order to make sense of life. We can get caught up in such a system for many years and successfully ignore our own impermanence.

But this detour eventually comes to an end when life still brings challenges to navigate and we are no longer able to deny the reality of change. The ultimate spiritual goal is to face up to our own impermanence and keep it always in our awareness, even as we pursue our chosen belief systems. Then we won't be using our beliefs to foster our denial of mortality.

Another detour that can sway you from the straightforward journey of the lesson of Impermanence is **authority**. If you manage to rise to a level of power within your community or workplace you can easily be seduced into believing that you have control over your circumstances. When other people take orders from you and policies are made or broken on your word it is natural to conclude that because you can manipulate certain outcomes in your sphere of influence you have power over all outcomes in life. Of course that is just another illusion but it can survive for years if you are able to maintain your position of authority. If you become accustomed to making decisions and taking control over situations you can be lulled into forgetting the nature of impermanence altogether.

But life will always circle around with a reminder for you about the real truths of existence: nothing lasts and everything changes. Sooner or later your little empire will begin crumbling at your feet, people will move on, laws will change, trends will go out of fashion, and you will be confronted once again with the impermanence of everything. This experience of watching things fall apart all around you gets repeated over and over again until you are finally ready to embrace the transient nature of all existence.

But before you reach that awareness you may continue to resist change and attempt to rebuild what seemed perfect in the past. Thus the detour of authority can last for many years. Look around society right now and you will see evidence everywhere of resistance to change and clinging to what was comfortable and familiar in the past. Evolution is the process of slowly wearing away this massive resistance so that impermanence can flow freely and bring about the necessary growth on the inward journey.

Finally a third detour that can distract us from the lesson of Impermanence is **projection,** which consists of externalizing our own inner fear onto other people so that it does not have to be experienced internally. In this situation for example, we might focus tirelessly on helping others who are dying so that we don't have to face our own fear of death. By keeping busy at all times and continually pointing out the fear in others, we can temporarily avoid looking at our own fear, which simmers deep within. But this detour can be rather short-lived because once again life itself will intervene and provide us with challenges that cannot be ignored and cannot be projected outwardly onto others.

When the illusion behind our detours becomes obvious to us it can be a very painful and unsettling time. For we will have spent countless hours, dollars and energy supporting a futile path instead of learning the skills and tools that might help us cope better with the transient nature of life. But the detours themselves are great learning experiences for us and as we recover from our traumas we emerge with new strength and new awareness that can prepare us for the next events of life.

THE EGO AND IMPERMANENCE

"It is not impermanence that makes us suffer.
What makes us suffer is wanting things to be permanent
when they are not."

-THICH NHAT HAHN

This quote by Thich Nhat Hahn perfectly describes the relationship of the ego toward the lesson of Impermanence—we simply want the things we love to stay the same as they have been. We resist the idea of change and cannot let go of the past because we find security in what we already know and are threatened by the unknown. Even when our current situation is not ideal we feel more comfortable with things as they are right now than facing uncertainty or transition. So energy is invested each day in maintaining the status quo and preserving the equilibrium of our lives. We seek support for keeping things the same as they are and find much validation in our society, which generally resists change, as well.

In some cases, the need for change can exert extreme pressure and we become depressed or anxious as a result of the inner demand for something different. Then the medical system offers us drugs to numb the call for change and help us stay firmly entrenched in the rut we have been occupying. While medications can offer some relief from the suffering we feel, the true remedy that is being called forth is to simply embrace the impermanence of all things and allow change to happen. We create our own misery by holding tightly to what we know and refusing to accept the unknown that is always flowing around and within us. This is a huge lesson for the ego to learn and can occupy most of a lifetime.

But change is inevitable in this human existence and ultimately cannot be denied; it arrives with or without our permission and disrupts everything that we have come to count on. The ego greets change with great sorrow because it has not yet learned the secret Thich Nhat Hahn teaches: "Thanks to impermanence everything is possible." The lower self can actually find purpose in life and bring about its highest meaning, not by resisting change, but by plunging headlong into the uncertainty and the mystery of life; by loosening the controls and allowing life to unfold in its own way. But this is not a natural awareness for the ego and does not come easily. There can be many years of frustration and misery in life while the ego tries repeatedly to prevent change from happening.

But Lama Yeshe reminds us "It is never too late. Even if you are going to die tomorrow, keep yourself straight and clear and be a happy human being today." Being "straight and clear" as he suggests, is simply allowing life to flow without trying to divert or interfere with the process. So impermanence becomes a reality for each of us, sometimes during the dying process or at the moment of our death, when we can no longer deny that change happens. But if your lower self can master this lesson before that time, you will discover unimaginable freedom and joy in your life, regardless of your circumstances.

TRAVEL ADVISORY

If we examine the behavior of a newly awakened ego that has just begun to perceive the truth, we can find, as with previous lessons, that the ego can also hijack the perception of impermanence. We have seen already that the ego can feign spiritual awareness in its attempt to control spiritual growth and protect itself from destruction. In this case the ego might seem to embrace the idea of impermanence but actually be promoting apathy and laziness instead. For the ego, the idea that nothing lasts and change must be accepted can lead to hopelessness and futility; why even bother if I can't do what I want? So the ego that is secretly in charge of the spiritual growth process might disguise passivity and inaction as impermanence. Rather than actively accept and embrace change the disguised ego just stops caring and pretends to be so enlightened that nothing matters any more.

But the truly evolved individual, under the guidance of the Soul, welcomes impermanence while still engaging fully with life and everything it offers. The difference is that energy flows continuously and freely when change is accepted, allowing synchronicities and "little miracles" to occur. When the hidden ego pretends that apathy is enlightenment, then the flow of energy is blocked, situations get tangled up, and solutions are difficult to find. Talking about the benefits of change while still trying to control things is a sure sign of an ego in disguise.

There is a delicate balance between accepting change whenever it comes yet remaining engaged and active in life, to make the most of every opportunity that arises.

Of course we all go through a similar process on our way to spiritual growth, with egos at various stages of awakening and letting go. So it is common when we dig deep within to discover our own hidden egoic motives underneath our attempts to be spiritual—this is in fact the way that we grow, one revelation at a time.

THE SOUL AND IMPERMANENCE

"Dissolver of sugar, dissolve me, if this is the time.
Do it gently with a touch of the hand, or a look...
Or do it suddenly like an execution.
How else can I get ready for death?"

-RUMI

Finally we are ready to hear the wisdom of the Soul and listen for the whispered guidance it can bring to our lives. For the Soul, impermanence is simply the way everything in the Universe operates. Change, including death of the physical form, is the foundation of all growth, everywhere. So the lesson of Impermanence is not to be feared, but to be celebrated since it is the key to life. The Soul never resists the flow of change but is fully within that flow, allowing everything to unfold in its own way, in its own time. There is nothing to fear for the Soul since every experience is a chance for growth and expansion. There is no negative or positive aspect to any change according to the Soul. Change "just is" and in fact is vital to everything in existence.

So the Soul or True Self takes a neutral view of every occurrence in life, even while the lower self tosses and turns with disappointment, regret, outrage, and sorrow over the changes that come along. The Soul glides along through each experience, finding openings and opportunities for *fearless love* to expand and spread.

The Soul actually longs to be "dissolved" as in Rumi's poem, for that act represents fully reintegrating with the Divine source. Death of the physical form is the ultimate dissolution as the body falls away and frees the Soul from its connection to Earth. While death is terrifying to the lower self, it is the final act of surrender and impermanence, by separating from the animating Soul and returning to the elemental aspect of Earth.

Since the Soul has no fear of impermanence or death it can guide us through the difficult changes we face in life.

The Soul offers us wisdom, inspiration, calmness and reassurance that all is well, the journey is unfolding just as it should. When we can open our minds and hearts to this guidance from the Soul we will finally possess the ability to navigate life's Suffering with Love, Forgiveness, Purpose, Presence, and Surrender. That is all we have come here for and all that really matters!

TRANSFORMING YOUR LIFE

We have reached the final lesson of this journey which will help you with all of the previous lessons as you spiral back through them over the course of your life. Understanding the reality of the impermanence of life will guide you through the current world as it falls apart in one way or another. There was never a time when things have not fallen apart and there never will be. This is how the universe works. When you grasp this underlying principle of life then you will face each new challenge with a growing level of equanimity.

Wherever you are on your journey, no matter what path you are pursuing, life will constantly show you its impermanence to help you learn this lesson. Take time to observe the destruction occurring on this planet, the systems that are breaking down, the divisions between people that are becoming apparent in our society. All of this falling apart is actually in service of whatever will arise next. Grieve the losses that are taking place—for they are real and significant—but don't get sidetracked into blame or despair. On this journey from ego to Soul you are here to shine the light of Divine wisdom and spread the fire of fearless love throughout the planet. Do your own inner work on a daily basis and go forth with all of your tools to be of service wherever life takes you.

TOOLS FOR THE JOURNEY

The fact that nothing lasts and everything changes is the ultimate lesson of the inward journey. Impermanence means that everything is always somewhere in the process of falling apart. And all creativity, evolution and growth are possible only because of the Impermanence of all things. When we can embrace the fact that only *fearless love* survives we can live with more ease and grace and all of the previous six lessons of this journey become more manageable. Therefore the tools for this lesson are some of the most important because they will support you at every other step along the way. Check the **Resources** page for these and other tools at www. eoluniversity.com/resources.

Mindset Shift

A helpful Mindset Shift as you grapple with the concept of Impermanence is to remember that change, especially death, is actually the driving force behind all of life. Nothing in this universe lasts, and everything in existence depends on the creative cycle of life and death. The impermanence of all things actually works in your favor because even your pain will eventually go away. Write about these questions in your journal:

- What frightens me most about the idea that nothing lasts?
- What is causing me the greatest suffering in my life right now?
- When in the past has my suffering gone away?
- If nothing in my life is going to last, then what really

matters?

SHADOW WORK

On your **Life Journey Map** make note of times when great changes or losses that have caused you deep pain have occurred in your past. Then explore each of those events in your journal using the 3 steps of Shadow work:

1. Recognize: What pain do I carry now over these losses of the past? How have I refused to allow these events to change me as a person?

2. Recover: Where has my path taken me after losses have occurred? What new things have I discovered as a result of my losses?

3. Rise Above: How can I remember that "this too shall pass" when I am in the midst of suffering? How can I view the Universe as a beneficent place where I am cared for? How might I use my creativity to help me when everything falls apart?

Example: *My father's suicide death was the loss that inflicted the most pain of my life and nearly destroyed me. Over time I needed to see that it helped me find my way to a new career in hospice and new growth as a spiritual being. The wisdom I learned from that pain has helped me in every other difficult situation I have encountered.*

PRACTICE

One Practice that will help you embrace Impermanence is

to do a **Death Meditation** each day. While this may sound morbid or frightening, it is simply a process to embrace the fact that no one knows when death will come and we should all be prepared for it at any moment. The meditation consists of using this simple mantra as you breathe in and out: "I might die today." Repeat it with each breath and allow this reality to sink into your thoughts and change your perspective. After you complete the meditation journal about some of the issues that have arisen during the day in light of this mantra. For example: I might die today so does the fact that someone took my parking space really matter? Or: I might die today so is it important that the grocery store ran out of my favorite cereal? Let this death meditation help you broaden your perspective on life.

ACTION STEP

As an Action Step for this lesson schedule at least one **Impermanence Activity** during which you can contemplate the fleeting nature of everything in existence. Consider watching the sunset one evening as you reflect on the passing of the day, draw a picture in the sand and watch the waves slowly erase it, watch a small fire die to become embers, drop flower petals or leaves into a stream and see them be carried by the water, or create a small gathering of leaves and sticks outside and watch as the breeze blows them away. Wherever you live you should be able to think of an activity in nature that will help you experience something coming to an end. During this time remain conscious of the fact that this event is happening "just for now" and will never be repeated in exactly the same way again. Enjoy each moment as time slips through your hands and then journal about the experience later.

10. THE SOUL-GUIDED LIFE

*"Those who don't feel this love pulling them like a river,
those who don't drink dawn like a cup of spring water,
those who don't want to change,
let them sleep."*

-RUMI

This inward journey of *fearless love*, as the ego discovers the Soul, is a path that no one really chooses, yet no one who is called to it can ultimately refuse. Like a raft on a rushing river we are swept along through life's currents, facing dangerous rapids at times and floating in still pools at other times. Life teaches us to navigate this flow by thrusting us into the middle of the stream—we learn the lessons we need as we tumble from one experience to another. But many people remain asleep, oblivious to the beauty of dawn and resistant to the pull of love. Rumi wisely advises us to let those people sleep. It's not our job to awaken them from slumber because we don't understand the timing or direction of their paths. We cannot stop the flow of change in our own lives, nor can we force change for someone else.

My discovery at the little shelter clinic was that Love is the ultimate reason for our existence and the highest expression of our purpose. If we simply continue to love those who come into our lives—whether they are awake or asleep, and whether we have a lifetime with them or just one brief encounter—then we are contributing our best and highest potential to the flow of *fearless love* in the Universe, and that is all we are asked to do. Though we might spend much of our time pursuing detours and getting caught in the traps of the ego, still we are learning and growing through each and every experience. Life itself teaches us everything we need to know, especially when we are open to any lesson and embrace the suffering along with the joy.

But the inward journey itself does not get easier no matter how much we have learned. As Rumi wrote: "Today, like every other day, we wake up empty and frightened ... Let the beauty we love be what we do."

Each day is a new beginning and we must discover over and over again how to hold steady in love while circumstances shift and fall apart all around us.

Gradually we learn to keep our focus on love alone but love leads us directly into greater challenges.

This is the hard work of spiritual growth and, contrary to certain teachings of the New Age, there is no *external* bliss or utopia to be found as you become more enlightened. Bliss is an *internal* state that can be attained at times but only arises from the inward journey through adversity, just as the lotus blossom grows only from the mud. Bliss is the tiny pine seedling that sprouts after a devastating forest fire or the flower that blooms in the aftermath of a volcano's destruction or the crystal that sparkles only when a geode has been broken apart. Embrace the suffering of life in order to experience the joy and the "little miracles" it provides. Let *fearless love* pull you on this expedition into unknown territory and find out what awaits you there.

ROADMAP FOR THE JOURNEY

"As you start to walk out on the way, the way appears."

-RUMI

Once you start the inward journey of awakening to the True Self or Soul, the path will begin to unfold before you, step by step. You won't be able to plan or control it, even though you will certainly try. Though your destination is unknown and your exact route has not been determined, you can still benefit from the guidance of the 7 lessons we reviewed in the earlier chapters. Mastering these lessons is the key to keeping your focus on love and you will be given many opportunities to learn them along the way.

After you have encountered all 7 lessons on your journey you can begin to utilize the wisdom from each of them to help you negotiate the challenges that life brings to you. You will become more skilled at coping with the ups and downs of this existence and bounce back from your difficulties more quickly if you have these tools available. They can be the pole stars in the night sky from which you navigate your course, one step at a time. Keep this wisdom at hand so you can turn to it when you need it most. To summarize the 7 lessons we will revisit them in reverse order so that you can see how they might be helpful to you in your growth process.

When you have begun to grasp the lesson of **Impermanence**, the fact that nothing lasts and everything changes, your relationship to the world, other people and life itself will start to shift. You will recognize that everything in your awareness at this moment is only temporary, including the difficulties you are experiencing right now. A tremendous sense of freedom will arise when you know that you cannot control most of what happens outside of you—your only real domain of power is within yourself. You will stop trying to force life to go the way you want it to and just relax into the flow that already exists. You will possess the knowledge you need in order to address any situation you encounter, as Rumi states: "Do not worry if all the candles in the world flicker and die ... we have the spark that starts the fire." Your fear of the unknown, including death, will lessen as you stop clinging even to life itself.

Once you are comfortable with allowing everything to constantly change in your day-to-day existence it will become much easier to **Surrender** to whatever life brings your way. Your expectations will diminish and you will be able to see every occurrence as a fascinating opportunity for growth, without judging it as "good" or "bad." This perspective will provide great comfort as you cope with loss for you will be able to find deep meaning within every experience. You will stop seeing life's difficulties as senseless or tragic, but will recognize the hidden gem of awareness that accompanies each problem.

As you become increasingly able to let go of expectations for the future you will begin to recognize that the **Purpose** of your life is to be exactly who you are. You will no longer see your occupation as the sole meaning of your existence but instead will view it as a vehicle for expressing your full potential. You will be less attached to the work you do and find more freedom to explore other options that allow you to be your best self. This new expanded definition of your life's purpose allows room for every possibility so you will no longer feel disappointed when things don't turn out as you had hoped and will never again see yourself as a failure. No matter what happens you will be fulfilling your purpose because you are always moving toward your best and highest potential.

After you are free from striving to accomplish a specific purpose for your life you will find it much easier to practice being in the **Present Moment**. You will begin to appreciate the beauty that exists all around you as you recognize that only this moment, right here, right now is real. It will become easier for you to focus your attention fully on whatever you are doing in the present without becoming distracted by regrets over the past or worries for the future. Once your energy is available to you in the present moment you will become more open to creativity, joy, love and even miracles, which exist only in the here and now. You will also discover that you already possess exactly what you need for this moment—there is nothing lacking. With this new awareness you will experience deep contentment with life, and discover that everything is perfect just as it is.

When you become fully focused and aware in the present moment you will find an increased desire to practice **Forgiveness**. In fact letting go of past resentments and anger will come naturally to you because there is no reason to carry the heavy burdens of the past into this present moment. What happened before is already done and you can finally release those old memories. As you begin to forgive all the pain and suffering of the past you will find more and more energy available to you for creativity in the present moment, which allows for even more forgiveness. You will also begin to heal your own Shadow wounds as they can now emerge as events from the past that simply need to be acknowledged and embraced.

Once you have begun to forgive others in your life for all of the transgressions of the past, your capacity for **Love** will become greatly increased. You will be able to cherish those closest to you more deeply than ever before because your heart will no longer be blocked by old resentment and pain. The deeper you love, the more you will need to practice forgiveness; the more you forgive the more energy you will be able to focus in the present moment. Thus you will cycle through these lessons, growing in both depth and breadth as your Soul continues to expand and generate love for the entire Universe.

Finally, after mastering these six lessons, your entire experience of **Suffering** will have been transformed. In fact you will no longer view life's challenges as suffering because you will have redefined them as opportunities for your growth. So, while life will continue to present you with difficulties from which to learn and grow, you will not experience suffering in the same way as in the past. Now you will possess the deep capacity for *fearless love* that is necessary to meet these struggles head on and the creativity to find the greatest potential and purpose in any situation. Your newly developed skills of forgiveness and surrender will be useful to you as you face the impermanence of this world without resentment or fear.

Thus these 7 lessons of Suffering, Love, Forgiveness, Present Moment, Purpose, Surrender, and Impermanence all work together and intertwine throughout life, enhancing one another and continually assisting you on your inward journey.

Gradually, as your True Self or Soul expands, your lower self finds greater comfort in yielding to the guidance of its counterpart. When tragedy does occur, love is available through the Soul to provide wisdom and solace and counteract the pain, while the other tools help guide the journey through suffering.

> **In fact, the Soul is the channel for Divine Love, which is the ultimate purpose of existence: to manifest this *fearless love* in all its diversity and splendor.**

When the True Self flourishes, love expands and life flows. This is the greatest secret of all for living with joy and fulfillment but it can take a lifelong inward journey for the lower self to discover this simple truth.

LOVE SHINES THROUGH THE DARKNESS

"This is how I would die into the love I have for you:
as pieces of cloud dissolve in sunlight."

-RUMI

My own inward journey from self to Soul began long ago at age 16 after the death of my friend Jolene with the epiphany that Love is the purpose of my life. As I tried to follow that guidance I encountered many difficulties along the way in both my personal and professional life. Each time I forgot my guidance or questioned its validity I was shown the way back to Love over and over again. Each time I was shattered by the twists and turns of life I found that Love was the only thing that could help me put the pieces back together again. In this final story, once more, Love found a way to break through the darkness and shine the light that was needed, like the sun's rays opening the clouds so we can finally see clearly.

BREAKING THROUGH THE CLOUDS

Several years after saying farewell to the shelter clinic and restarting life in a new community, I would be reminded once again of the Love Project and its "little miracles." I had fully adjusted to the next stage of my medical career, working in a clinic for low-income, uninsured individuals and occasionally volunteering for our tiny local hospice. Life had settled into a comfortable routine, but as always happens in this impermanent world, everything was about to change.

One afternoon I arrived home from work to receive a phone call that my cousin Jolene had died of a sudden and unexpected cardiac arrest. I was in shock to learn that Jolene was gone at such a young age just as my friend Jolene had also left this planet too soon many years before. My cousin was one year younger than me and we had been close friends growing up because we lived just a few doors apart on the same street.

Hearing the devastating news of her death I was flooded with memories of our childhood together: making mud pies and selling them in our outdoor "bakery," creating elaborate Barbie villages and imaginary doll hospitals, restaurants, and theaters. I couldn't believe that I would never see her again. Jolene had always been one of my favorite people but we had grown apart in adulthood when our lives took us in different directions. We had reconnected briefly when my father died and she opened her home to my family and me while we struggled through his funeral and memorial service. Her kindness was a bright light for me during those terrible dark days.

Then I recalled with a shudder of guilt that Jolene had invited me to join her for coffee on my last visit home, just a few months before her death, but my schedule was "too busy" and I had turned her down. Now I was filled with regret that I had missed my last opportunity to connect with her before she died. Even though I couldn't have known that I would never see her again, I should not have passed up the chance to spend time with her. I had learned over and over again through my hospice work that life has no guarantees and should never be taken for granted. By failing to follow my own wisdom I had deprived of us both of a final goodbye and my heart ached with remorse over my thoughtless decision.

As I drove home for the funeral I thought about the fact that I had only known two Jolenes in my life and now both of them had died before I was ready to let them go. When I arrived at the church for the memorial I found my relatives to be in the same state of shock and disbelief that I was experiencing. We gathered together in the mourners' room before the service began, saying very little and staring at the floor with the sounds of organ music and shuffling feet outside the door.

Finally, Jolene's niece sat down next to me and asked "Why won't anyone talk about what has happened? This is going to change everything in our lives, forever."

She was right—everything had changed in a most unbelievable and unacceptable way, but that was why no one could say anything at that moment. Our minds were trying to fathom this new reality and wondering how we could go on for even one more day after such a devastating loss.

Following the memorial service we drove in a long procession to Jolene's family home on a small ranch outside of town where the reception was being held. Hundreds of people had come to say farewell to her and I wondered briefly how we would all fit inside one house. But I had forgotten that she and her husband had recently built a massive log home on their property with a huge landscaped yard so there was ample space for all of her friends and family.

The ranch looked beautiful that August day with trees and flower gardens in full bloom surrounding the massive house that held a surprise for me when I walked inside the front door. There amidst the rustic wooden furniture and mountain-inspired décor I saw dozens and dozens of bears everywhere I looked. There were stuffed Teddy bears of all colors and sizes, paintings of bears, sculptures of bears, a tapestry depicting bears, and bear-shaped pillows, vases, and figurines. Jolene had been collecting bears for years and her entire house was filled with them.

In that moment, while feeling such tender grief over Jolene's death I was also filled with memories of Charlotte and her Teddy bears, the shelter clinic, the Love Project, and all the little miracles that had taken place during those years. Tears came to my eyes as I contemplated how life had changed over the past decade and how much I missed the people I would never see again and the experiences that were gone forever. Life is both sweet and painful as it brings us one challenge after another—all in the name of growth. Sometimes it seems too much to endure.

While I was suffering with my deep feelings of regret over refusing an opportunity to see Jolene earlier that year, I also knew that others were experiencing even deeper pain. Jolene's husband and her three children, her parents, brother and sister-in-law, nieces and nephews, friends and neighbors, all were dealing with an enormous hole in their lives that had once been filled by Jolene's loving presence. Since I hadn't seen her for several years and she wasn't part of my day-to-day life, I would not miss her with the same intense pain that they were facing.

As I stood inside Jolene's house holding onto one of her Teddy *bears, I was filled with even more regret and confusion because I realized I'd made choices in my life that had taken me away from her many years before. There was no way to go back, no way to recover any of the time that had not been spent with her ... time that had also not been given to any of the members of my original family ... the same time that I had not given to my father in the years before he died. That day my heart ached with grief and guilt and my mind reeled with thoughts of all the decisions we make for our lives and the consequences we cannot anticipate. There was no way to predict any of these feelings so many years ago when I left home to pursue a medical career. No way to know that it could hurt so much to have left behind every person I once loved in order to fulfill what I believed to be my purpose. These are the painful trade-offs life hands to us along the way.*

Somehow each of us who loved Jolene came together that day in her exquisite home and managed to muddle through the over-whelming pain of saying goodbye to her. Somehow we kept going and kept living our lives, even though everything was upside down and turned inside out. Somehow we all kept loving one another and looking after each other's broken hearts and we got through that day, then the next day, and the next, as life continued to move on.

But one year later the same group of people that had mourned together that awful day traveled once again down the dirt road that led to Jolene's home. This time we were gathering to celebrate the wedding of her son: a joyous occasion in the midst of ongoing unspeakable grief, a joining together in the midst of total brokenness. Each of us was determined to smile and celebrate the great joy of this wedding but our hearts were aching at the thought of how much Jolene would have wanted to be there to see her oldest child marry his love. Jolene had always been a great social organizer, hosting spectacular parties and events for friends and family. In fact she had been helping her son and his fiancée plan this very wedding at the time of her death.

Almost overwhelmed by the conflicting emotions that flooded us, we came once again to the huge house that now seemed so lonely without Jolene's love and laughter to fill it. The wedding was to be held outside on the vast lawn where a gazebo had been decorated with flowers and rows of white plastic chairs were trimmed with white balloons. But the sky had been filled with thick black clouds all day, threatening a downpour that could potentially drench the entire wedding party. The air was so heavy with the impending rain that it seemed unlikely the ceremony could be completed before the storm broke, which only added to the sadness that weighed heavily on our hearts.

To pass the time before the bride and groom arrived, my aunt asked me to take a walk with her around the yard. She wanted to show me a memorial garden that had been built a few months before to honor Jolene. There on a stone terrace was an outdoor fireplace, lovely flower gardens, and a platform holding a brass sculpture that had been commissioned in Jolene's memory by her husband. It was a mother bear, fast asleep, with three cubs nestling up to her while she slumbered peacefully. Of course the fact that it was a sculpture of bears was perfect—Jolene would have loved it. I was moved to tears by the thought that this sleeping mother bear would never again awaken to cuddle her little ones to her breast and look after their rambunctious play.

Once again I felt the black hole of grief inside of me that mirrored the dark threatening sky overhead. But somehow I had to pull myself together, paste the smile back on my face and get ready to celebrate love and life on this special day.

My aunt and I returned to the front yard and were ushered to our seats as it was finally time for the wedding to begin. The white helium-filled balloons that had been tied to each of the chairs floated valiantly on their fragile ribbons as they were battered from side-to-side by the wind, which again echoed the turbulent grief that raged in our hearts but could not be spoken.

At one point during the ceremony the minister paused in the midst of his sermon and laid his notes on the nearby altar. As he looked out at the faces of the attendees, the same people he had addressed at Jolene's funeral one year earlier, he spoke softly and informally as if in private conversation with each one of us.

"I know how hard this is. I know that each one of you is missing Jolene right now. She would have loved this wouldn't she—being part of this beautiful celebration and the party that will follow?"

A ripple of nervous laughter went through the crowd, accompanied by a noticeable sigh of relief as someone had finally spoken the truth that none of us could bear to mention. At last we were able to acknowledge the pain that was screaming for our attention in the middle of this joyful celebration.

Next the minister asked us to untie the white balloons that were attached to our chairs and hold the ribbons in our hands. He said a blessing for our broken, grieving hearts. He asked for peace and healing for us that day and that we each remember that Jolene was not far away—she was smiling down on this beautiful celebration with all of her love for us.

When he ended his prayer he instructed us to release the balloons we were holding and let go of our pain, as well. We looked up and watched as hundreds of white balloons rose together higher and higher in the sky—carrying away our pain and transporting our love to Jolene.

After a few moments the balloons appeared to coalesce at a point just below the threatening rainclouds. Then they rose together, radiating a brilliant white sheen against the blackness of the clouds. In the next instant, the balloons touched the edge of the cloud-bank and miraculously split the thunderhead in two to reveal the blue sky and sunshine that had previously been obscured. The balloons continued their upward journey as the clouds quickly dissipated and rays of sunlight streamed down upon us.

The entire congregation gasped at this incredible sight as we continued to gaze up at the sky, now with brilliantly lit faces, shining with love and joy at the miracle we had just observed.

"Jolene is truly right here with us," the minister reminded us again and concluded the ceremony while we looked on in amazement.

The reception was held inside a huge tent that was no longer necessary because the threatening storm had completely moved out of the area. At every table there was excited talk of the astonishing scene we had just witnessed with comments like "That was so 'Jolene!'" and "She was determined to be part of this wedding one way or another!"

Laughter flowed freely and we danced and celebrated that night —still missing our dear Jolene but feeling her presence again, more powerfully than ever before. Our grief and pain were still with us, but tempered now with this spectacular memory of Jolene's light and love that we would never forget. We were able to support the newly-weds and cheer for their happiness with genuine joy as all our clouds of dark pain had been lifted away for that moment.

Several years later, that wedding miracle is still talked about with reverence and awe, as the day when Jolene came to us to dispel our gloom and grief and remind us that love is always to be cherished and celebrated. As for me however, I continued to carry traces of guilt and regret over my failure to visit her that one last time while she was alive, until one night when she came to me in a dream.

In the dream I was attending a wedding reception where the guests were all seated at round tables, eating dinner. I looked up from my plate and saw Jolene walk into the room and directly toward me. We hugged and held each other as I rejoiced in this opportunity to see her once again. She asked if she could sit with me and hovered next to me while I ate my dinner. When I asked if she wanted me to show her the table where her parents and children were seated, she responded, "No, I can't go to them yet. It's not time. I can only be here with you."

When I awoke from the dream I knew for certain that Jolene had visited me and that she was still looking in on all of us. I felt her vast unconditional love through the dream and understood that she came to offer me forgiveness and heal my guilt over not visiting her. In fact she was holding all of her loved ones in her presence and assisting us on our painful journeys here. It was clear that she was watching over her family even though it was too soon for her to connect with them. I had a sense that they would be able to experience her presence when the burden of grief they were carrying lightened enough to make room for her gentle essence.

Finally, a few years later I would once again be reminded of Jolene when my husband and I were shopping for a picture to hang in our bedroom. We were browsing through a nature photographer's gallery where his assistant was showing us his work and describing how he had captured each image. She brought us to a large framed photo that had the exact proportions we needed for our bedroom wall.

It was a mountain scene and in the foreground there was a mother bear walking through a meadow with three cubs following her while rays of sunlight illuminated them against the black backdrop of the mountainside. The assistant told us that it is rare for a mother bear to give birth to triplets so when the photographer spotted that family he knew he had to get a picture. He had tracked them for hours but there were dark storm clouds covering the entire sky and threatening to burst at any moment, so the lighting wasn't right for the photo. But just as he had decided to give up his quest, the clouds suddenly and inexplicably dissipated to reveal just enough blue sky and sunshine to create this perfectly lit scene.

As I stood in the middle of the studio, in front of this photograph of the mother bear and her three cubs illuminated by rays of sunlight that had unexpectedly penetrated black storm clouds, I suddenly began to cry with powerful heaving sobs that I could not control. From deep within me all of the remnants of grief and pain I had been carrying for years and years came to the surface to finally be released. All of the sorrow of my entire life seemed to rush forward as I wailed in a way I had never done before. Of course the clerk was concerned and uncomfortable with my weeping, having never before seen such a display of emotion inside that gallery.

She offered a weak attempt to help by saying, "Well it is a nice picture ...."

But still my tears didn't stop. Finally we paid for the photograph and left so that I could continue to cry in a more private space.

I was embarrassed that I had expressed such emotion in public but I couldn't stop the deluge of pain that had welled up inside and I knew that this was a pivotal moment of my life. This was one incredible instant when all of the stars and planets aligned and every experience of my past suddenly fell into place as the perfect manifestation of the entire reason for my existence.

I couldn't explain it, but everything that had happened suddenly made sense to me: my father's suicide, my hospice work, the little shelter clinic, Teddy bears, moving away, Charlotte's death, the deaths of my two Jolenes ... every death I had faced. All of these experiences of my life had been connected together by invisible threads of love. It was so clear in that moment that we are all walking beneath dark storm clouds every day, wondering when the rain will deluge us. Most of the time we cannot see the perfect light hidden behind the clouds that shines down with love in every single moment.

We are wandering in darkness of our own making, confused and in pain. But there is nothing but love for us here waiting for any opportunity to illuminate our lives. Waiting to shower us with "little miracles" and tender moments, magical relationships that come and go, and every little thing that we need on our journey here.

The only thing we don't know, that we cannot see most of the time, is that everything is perfect, just as it is. That's the one thing we spend our entire lives searching for and it is right in front of us all the *time. This crazy, mixed-up, painful, outrageous, joyful, frustrating life is actually perfect in every way.*

WHEN SELF MEETS SOUL

> *"Moonlight floods the whole sky from horizon to horizon. How much it can fill your room depends on its windows."*

-RUMI

This final story illustrates how over and over again in life we are brought to the moment when the lower self recognizes the shining light of the Soul and is awed by the Divine wisdom and love that have been available all along. Our small and cloudy "windows" prevent us from being fully illuminated by this light much of the time, but it is always there, always ready to offer clarity to any situation. Each time a ray of light pierces through the dimness we remember once again that we are actually Souls on an inward journey of love here on planet Earth.

The lower self is a necessary companion for the Soul, providing transportation and sensory input for this adventure, but a self that is unaware of its true purpose can wander and struggle through an entire lifetime while it ignores the ever-present guidance within.

The Soul clothes itself in a physical form to experience the impermanence of Earth, to learn to suffer and surrender and thus discover the deepest possible love that can be manifested on a planet such as this.

To give and receive love in human form is the entire reason for this project of the Soul—so simple and so difficult at once.

In each lifetime the lower self, oblivious to this information, must take the journey to discover again the Soul that has been present always and forever, shining light and whispering guidance that cannot be perceived. But when the windows have been polished just enough and the light suddenly bursts through, the pull of love is so powerful that no one can resist. Then the inward journey begins—you step out on the path of your true purpose and begin your own quest for spiritual growth.

THE PATH WITH HEART

"A warrior chooses a path with heart, any path with
    heart,
and follows it; and then he rejoices and laughs.
He knows because he sees that his life will be over
    altogether too soon.
He sees that nothing is more important than anything
    else."

-CARLOS CASTANEDA

You must become a warrior as you travel along the path of your true purpose—your path with heart. Life will present you with just enough challenge and adversity to further your growth during this short sojourn on planet Earth so be ready for anything. The 7 lessons are the tools that will help you master each difficulty and glean every bit of wisdom available to you from each experience.

First you will learn to **manage your own Suffering**. A warrior faces difficulty head-on and goes straight into the fire of the dragon. Fearlessness will serve you well when you encounter illness, loss, disappointment, failure, and frustration. Take responsibility for your own life, even though you are not the cause of your troubles; your longing for growth in love and joy has brought you the perfect challenges to take you deeper into yourself. So don't run away, place blame on anyone or anything else, or get lost in despair. This pain you are facing now is what your Soul came here to experience so make the most of it; maximize your own potential by rising above each challenge. To do this you will need some skills for assistance like taking the Galaxy View, quieting thoughts, calming the emotions, and opening the heart. Develop your own daily "warrior practice" to strengthen your courage and train your mind to listen for the Soul's guidance.

Next you will **focus on relationships** because connecting with others is one of the fundamental tasks of the Soul on planet Earth. The wisdom of **Love** can only be learned through experience so begin to see the opportunities for sharing love that already exist in your life. Love flows when it is given first and then received in return so make it a priority to reach out to others with compassion rather than seeking to be loved by others. When you prioritize *giving* love over *receiving* love you will find that you always have enough to share as long as you care for yourself at the same time. If you feel lonely or needy for love from someone else it is a sign that your "windows" are too small or too cloudy to take in the Divine love that is always available to you.

Practice self-love by healing the wounds that you carry and embracing your own Shadow, which will require you to become a master of **Forgiveness**, as well. When you forgive yourself, others, life, and God for the pain of your past, you release the energy that has been tied up for years maintaining old memories of anger, resentment, grief, and guilt. Forgiveness helps you clean the "windows" so you can bring more light inside and expand your capacity to love even more. Cultivate your own regular practice of forgiveness so that you can continually clear out old negative energy and make room for more *fearless love* to flow in your life.

Next on this "path with heart" you will **consider the work** you do on a daily basis to help you survive physically here on this planet. This includes the time you spend at your job and also the effort you put forth outside of your employment, both at home and in your community. The most important determinant of productivity in all of your work is your ability to be in the **Present Moment**. By focusing your attention on what is right here and right now, you can face each task in front of you one-step-at-a-time and not be overwhelmed by the size of your to-do list. You will be more efficient in any work you undertake if you are not distracted by past issues or future worries.

So your ability to stay in the present moment will enhance the quality and ease of everything you do and allow you to fulfill your ultimate **Purpose**. As mentioned before, the purpose for your existence is less about the details of your career path itself and more about who you are becoming as you pursue your career. Your choice of work will define the activities you perform each day and shape the experiences life brings to you for your growth. But your mindset and spiritual awareness will determine how you fulfill your own inner potential within that work. You can be "a warrior on a path with heart" whether you function as a janitor or a CEO, a stockbroker or a relief worker. *How* you show up for your job each day will make all the difference: be fully present, give your best effort to the work at hand, have an open heart and mind, and bring love to every situation and experience. When you operate from that perspective in everything you do, you will be manifesting your highest potential and fulfilling your true purpose.

Finally, on your warrior path, you will **develop your spiritual skills** to support your ongoing growth and evolution. As part of this process you will learn to let go of your expectations and stop trying to control the future. When you **Surrender** to the wisdom of life itself you will learn to trust the guidance that comes to you from your Soul in every moment. By giving up the tendency of your ego/mind to try to manipulate a certain outcome, you will relax into the flow of events and find peace even when things don't go the way you had envisioned. You will also become much more resilient to the unexpected occurrences of life and will be able to cope better with the natural physical challenges that accompany aging.

As you embrace the entire cycle of life and death you will begin to cherish the reality of **Impermanence**: that within this physical realm on planet Earth, everything changes and nothing lasts. You will recognize that only your Soul, which whispers to you constantly, will continue on after everything else that defines you dissolves away. Thus, each moment of your life will become precious and you will be filled with motivation to enjoy everything that comes to you without squandering any part of this sacred physical existence. On your path with heart you will take things lightly and laugh at the serendipitous and paradoxical nature of the Universe. You will be fully open to receive a constant flow of Divine love and to share it with everyone, everywhere you go, without worrying about how it all turns out. You will trust that somehow everything is perfect in its own way, including you and your unique warrior path. Incorporate spiritual rituals like meditation and prayer into your daily "warrior practice" to still your mind and nourish your Soul.

THE SPIRAL TURNS

*"You were born with wings,
why prefer to crawl through life?"*

-RUMI

And so we have come full circle on this inward journey of the self to discover the Soul: the Divine companion that has always been waiting within. After years of struggle—crawling through life's arid deserts, stumbling over precarious mountain passes, and slogging through the muddy swamps of human existence—we arrive where our journey started, finally able to recognize that the wings of the Soul were present all along, always ready to lift us up from the suffering of planet Earth. Now our travels continue as we follow the spiral deeper and deeper into the lessons of life and death. We do not stop growing once we become acquainted with our own Soul, in fact, that is when the true journey of enlightenment begins.

Now with open hearts and minds we can be filled with the

light that the world desperately needs. We can offer our physical presence as a tool of the Divine for showing the way to those still lost in the dark, for healing the wounded hearts of our fellow travelers, and for continuously unraveling our own secrets that remain hidden within. This is the path that will take us one day through the ultimate dissolution of the body/mind/ego—everything that arises from this point on is here to teach us how to consciously let go of this physical existence.

As you face your own aging and eventual death, your Soul will be your comforter, your physician, your guide, and your faithful companion, with sturdy wings to carry you through.

This is the true reason for the journey to discover the Soul, the true purpose of your life on Earth: to learn to cherish every precious moment of physical existence with your entire being and then to let it slip lightly through your hands when your final breath is exhaled.

TRANSFORMING YOUR LIFE AND THE PLANET

The work you've been invited to do through these pages consists of unearthing your Shadow, taming your ego, and receiving the guidance of your Soul. As mentioned over and over again you will need to commit to this path and intentionally work on it every day if you want to grow spiritually. While you are free to refuse the path and wait until your deathbed to consider these issues, you will continue to feel the pull of love throughout your life, coaxing you into the flow like a river drawing you down-stream. Life will continue falling apart, as it always does, and you will have endless opportunities to do this work. But step-ping onto the inward path now will not only change everything for you, it will also change this planet and all of the life forms it supports.

While our own individual existence is threatened by unex-plored Shadow elements and untamed ego drives, the entire world is also susceptible to those same negative forces. We see all around us the desecration of the planet and its resources, racial injustice, income inequality, political corruption, exploita-tion of power, and widespread hatred and violence amongst our fellow humans. The daily news is filled with disheartening and nearly unbearable stories as things fall apart all around us. We cannot change much of what happens in the world, but we can change ourselves spiritually and any effort we exert will have a positive impact on the planet.

The HeartMath Institute has done research for years showing that when we create "coherence" between our mind and heart (ego and Soul) we increase the electromagnetic field of the heart and the ability to spread love and peace to the planet. The more people who achieve this state of coherence, the greater the effect on society as a whole. Indeed studies have shown that when large groups of people meditate simultane-ously there have been significant measurable drops in crime and violence in the community.[1] Every change you make, every step you take on your inward journey from ego to Soul can influence the world around you for the better. Let's get started.

THERE IS ONLY LOVE

*"Whatever happens just keep smiling
and lose yourself in Love....
Love is the bridge between you and everything."*

-RUMI

For all of the wise words and inspiring stories and compelling lessons brought forth in this book, there is only one thing you need to remember: Love ... just love. If you keep your focus always on love you will find your way through any difficulty. If you remember to act with love in every relationship you can heal any painful situation. If you let love guide your choices you will stay on the path with heart—the path that will lead you ultimately to discover everything you need for this lifetime. If you fill each moment of your life with love then you will arrive at the moment of your death with a peaceful heart and mind. You will have no need to cling to physical existence or delay your passage into the light. We are born into this life on Earth so that we can learn these things: to love unconditionally through suffering and pain, to find joy in the midst of impermanence, and to leave behind the beauty as well as the burden of physical existence when the time comes to travel into the next realm.

While it appears to us during our time on Earth that we are on a finite journey in these physical body/minds we inhabit, we are actually Souls on an eternal path through the mysteries of the Universe. We will never stop traveling or learning or growing as spiritual beings and there is comfort in that knowledge, even though we agonize and weep and break apart over every loss we experience here on the physical plane.

Ultimately we will lose everything tangible we have come to love on planet Earth and yet all that we love will also remain part of us forever. If we can only remember that we are actually already One with everything in existence, then we will slip out of these physical bodies with ease at exactly the right time. Focus your attention on Love—when you are ill or injured, when you face the losses of aging, when your heart is broken, when death comes for those you cherish.

Love will guide you through the pain and illuminate the path for you to follow, one step at a time. Love transcends all suffering and loss and creates the "little miracles" of life. Indeed Love is what you are made from. Let Love be what really matters in your life through all time and all space .. for there is only Love.

The Tao of Death
Verse 51

Love—the Creative Energy of the Universe—
gives rise to everything
and then draws it back again
with perfect timing.

This is the Way of Death.

Love breathes life
into material form
and nurtures, teaches, and protects it,
asking nothing in return,
until life dissolves once again
into Love.

Knowing that your life is just
a single breath of Love,
cherish everything
cling to nothing.

The Way of Death
whispers in your ear:
"There is only Love."

-Karen Wyatt MD

NOTES

INTRODUCTION

1. https://youtu.be/UyyjU8fzEYU

2. WHEN EGO MEETS SOUL

1. *Integral Life Practice* – (Wilber, Patten, Leonard, Morelli, 2008)

4. THE SECOND LESSON: LOVE

1. https://rogermooreinstitute.com

5. THE THIRD LESSON: FORGIVENESS

1. http://fetzer.org/resources/fetzer-survey-love-and-forgiveness-american-society
2. http://greatergood.berkeley.edu/article/item/the_new_science_of_forgiveness
3. Front Hum Neurosci. 2013 Dec 9;7:839. doi: 10.3389/fnhum.2013.00839. eCollection 2013.
4. Explore (NY). 2005 May;1(3):169-76.

6. THE FOURTH LESSON: THE PRESENT MOMENT

1. https://rogermooreinstitute.com

10. THE SOUL-GUIDED LIFE

1. https://www.heartmath.org/research/science-of-the-heart/global-coherence-research/

ABOUT THE AUTHOR

KAREN WYATT MD spent years as a doctor caring for patients in challenging settings, such as hospices, nursing homes and indigent clinics before she left medicine to pursue a new career as an author, speaker, and podcaster. She draws on her years of medical experience in the stories she includes in her narrative non-fiction books, which focus on the everyday spiritual lessons we all need to learn in order to live our best lives.

She is the host of the popular End-of-Life University Podcast and has inspired thousands of people to find love and joy in the midst of difficult times. Check out her website at http://www.eoluniversity.com.

- facebook.com/kwyattmd
- twitter.com/spiritualmd
- instagram.com/kwyattmd
- youtube.com/eoluniversity
- linkedin.com/in/karen-wyatt-md-49723624
- patreon.com/eolu
- amazon.com/author/karenwyattmd

7 Lessons for Living from the Dying:

How to Nurture What Really Matters

A Matter of Life & Death:

Stories to Heal Loss & Grief

The Tao of Death:

The Secret to a Rich and Meaningful Life

Printed in Great Britain
by Amazon

57985216R00159